THE KID'S ADDRESS BOOK

D1319836

Other Books by Michael Levine

*The Address Book: How to
   Reach Anyone Who Is Anyone*

The Corporate Address Book

The Music Address Book

The Environmental Address Book

THE KID'S ADDRESS BOOK

Over 1,500 Addresses
of Celebrities, Athletes,
Entertainers, and More
. . . Just for Kids!

MICHAEL LEVINE

A Perigee Book
New York

Every effort has been made to provide the most current mailing addresses. Addresses, however, do change, and neither publisher nor author is responsible for misdirected or returned mail.

Perigee Books
are published by
The Putnam Publishing Group
200 Madison Avenue
New York, NY 10016

Copyright © 1992 by Michael Levine

All rights reserved. This book, or parts thereof,
may not be reproduced in any form without permission.
Published simultaneously in Canada

Library of Congress Cataloging-in-Publication Data

Levine, Michael, date.
    The kid's address book : over 1,500 addresses of celebrities,
athletes, entertainers, and more . . . just for kids! / Michael Levine.
        p.   cm.
    Summary: Provides the addresses of movie stars, athletes, clubs,
organizations, publications, musicians, and kid-related businesses
and products.
    ISBN 0-399-51783-9 (alk. paper)
    1. Celebrities—Directories—Juvenile literature.   2. Celebrities
—United States—Directories—Juvenile literature.   3. Letter-
writing—Juvenile literature.   [1. Celebrities—Directories.]
I. Title.
CT107.L52   1992   92-6815 CIP AC
920'.0025'73—dc20

Cover design by Richard Rossiter

Photograph of the author © 1992 by Debra Young

Printed in the United States of America

              6   7   8   9   10

This book is printed on acid-free paper.

A friend may well be reckoned the masterpiece of Nature.
—RALPH WALDO EMERSON

ACKNOWLEDGMENTS

I'm lucky. I get to say publicly to the special people in my life how much they mean to me. To each of them, my appreciation for their help with this book and, most of all, their unwavering friendship and love.

My brilliant literary agent and good friend, Alice Martell, and her assistant, Paul Raushenbush.

My friends at Putnam (where I have been published since 1984): Laura Shepherd, Eugene Brissie, and Jacqueline Foley.

My dedicated father, Arthur O. Levine, stepmother, Marilyn, and sister, Patty.

My stepson, Danny.

My loving new family (in-law), Karl and Gerri Engemann, Paul, Suzanne, Austin, Shannon, Ryan, and Bret Engemann.

My special friends Bart Andrews, Rana Bendixen and Sorrell, Ken Bostic, Leo Buscaglia, Bill Calkins, John Hess, Karen L'Heureux, Richard Impressia, Bette Geller Jackson, Ed and Jean King, Bonnie and Gordon Larson, Heather Lawrence, Richard Lawson, Nancy Mager, John McKillop, Lynn Novatt, Dennis Prager, Steven Short, Joshua Trabulus, Erline White.

My wonderful business partners, Mitchell Schneider and Monique Moss.

My office family, Jeff Albright, Todd Brodginski, Amanda Cagan, Marla Capra, Katherine Caulfield, Vivianna Ceballos, Stacey Glazer, Gail Holtzman, Kim Kaiman, Matt Labov, Carol Mannara, Julie Nathanson, Robert Pietranton, Tresa Redburn-Cody, Marcee Rondan, Jane Singer, Julie Wheeler, Staci Wolfe.

To my business associates Bob and Lori Bernstein, Laura Herlovich, Barry Langburg, Matt Lichtenberg, Sal Manna, Dan Pine, and Joy Sapieka.

Special thanks to Kathleen Conner for incredible commitment to excellence in the researching of this book.

For my wife,
Shawn,
who taught me that if there is anything better
than being loved, it is loving.

CONTENTS

AUTHOR'S NOTE TO KIDS

Dear Kids:

People are taught in America that you get to vote once a year. This is *not* true. In America you get to vote every day. The decisions about what you buy, where you eat, television shows you watch, music you listen to are all a form of voting. Additionally, your comments, suggestions, thoughts, and criticisms are a form of voting. It is my hope that young people will use this *Kid's Address Book* as a way of getting involved in the world and sharing your opinions with people all over the place.

While researching this book I found that nearly everyone I spoke with is anxious to hear from you. They want to understand how you feel and they don't want it sugar-coated. "I look forward to my letters from my fans because they tell me the truth," said one of the members of the group New Kids on the Block. "The more I read, the better I understand." As you write to people in this book you may be surprised to learn that people do respond. That's the exciting part, and you'll learn about that soon enough.

- **Here are several important things to remember in writing to famous people: Always include a self-addressed stamped envelope (SASE).** This is the single most important factor in writing a letter if you want a response. Because of the unusually high volume of mail notable people receive, anything you can do to make it easier for them to respond is going to work in your favor.
- **Keep your letters short and to the point.** Notables are usually extremely busy people, and long letters tend to be set aside for "future" consideration. For instance, if you want an autographed picture of your favorite TV personality, don't write three pages of prose to explain your request.
- **Make your letter as easy to read as possible.** This means type it or, at the very least, handwrite it very neatly. Avoid crayons, markers,

or even pencils. And don't forget to leave some margins on the paper. And be sure to include your name and address (even on all materials that you include with your letter) in the event the materials are separated from your letter. You would be amazed how many people write letters without return addresses and then wonder why they never hear from the person to whom they wrote.

- **Never send food to notables.** Due to spoilage and security matters, it cannot be eaten anyway. (Would you eat a box of homemade brownies given to you by a total stranger?) If you send gifts, don't wrap them in large boxes with yards of paper, string, and tape around them. (They may not have a crowbar on hand.)
- Again, don't forget to include your name and address on all material you send. And, of course, don't send—or ask for—money.

The most important thing is to get going and have fun with all of this. Keep a chart at home and monitor your results. Drop me a note and let me know how you are doing.

Michael Levine
KID'S ADDRESS BOOK
8730 Sunset Boulevard, 6th Floor
Los Angeles, CA 90069

P.S. Remember, a person who writes to another makes more impact than ten thousand who are silent.

AUTHOR'S NOTE TO PARENTS

The Kid's Address Book is more than a simple collection of names and addresses. It is actually a tool of empowerment for young people. Contained herein are all the essentials to instill in them a love for the lost art of letter-writing. Adults would be wise to engage in it as well, but how much more significant to inflame the next generation with a passion for writing.

The great American jurist Oliver Wendell Holmes once said, "Pretty much all the honest truth-telling there is, is done by children." But who's listening? Today, we see scholastic test scores at all grade levels on the decline, poverty rates for children on the rise, and increasing numbers of young people falling victim to the modern-day scourges of drugs, teenage pregnancy, crime, and general aimlessness.

Our kids are in trouble.

Or, more to the point, we are all in trouble if we cannot provide young people with a new direction, a sense of purpose, and a safer world in which to live. Most parents mean well, and strive to give their children a financial, educational, moral, and spiritual foundation. But today we bear witness to the Nintendo-ization of American youth. Unfortunately, the easiest way to get a kid's attention these days is to stand in front of the TV. Kids who spend an inordinate amount of time watching the tube will surely go down in history—not to mention math, science, and English.

We have abdicated much of our responsibility to guide our children properly. Into that vacuum have rushed pseudo-heroes like Arnold Schwarzenegger, whose violence-ridden films portray a menacing world of "kill or be killed"; or Madonna, whose lurid "boy toy" sexuality is expertly mimicked by ten-year-old girls. Surely we can do better than that.

One way is to acquaint children with their own inherent power. If they can, in some way, help fashion their own fates, and make a direct impact on the world around them, then they will come away with a restored sense of self-reliance and capability. They will become who they are, not what the media tell them they should be. One clear and effective way to do that is to teach our kids to write letters.

I call it the lost art of letter-writing. The contemporary essayist Paul Bowles once wrote:

> "In other centuries this [letter-writing] was taken for granted. Not any longer. Only a few people carry on true correspondences. No time, the rest tell you. Quicker to telephone. Like saying a photograph is more satisfying than a painting. There wasn't all that much time for writing letters in the past either, but time was found, as it generally can for whatever gives pleasure."

The element of pleasure is missing for most people when contemplating writing. If only they experienced the fun and gratification of letter-writing. Writing is nothing more than guiding a dream, and we all know how enjoyable dreams can be.

For kids, the trick is helping them comprehend that letter-writing will bring results. Although writing can be a pure pleasure in and of itself, writing letters is specifically designed to communicate to *someone else*. Implicit in the act of writing and sending a letter is the expectation that the addressee will read and respond. Corresponding is an active dialogue between the minds of two people. No, it's not as fast as calling, but I daresay the pen is mightier than the car phone.

Kids instinctively grasp this. I've known shy children barely able to look another human being in the eye, who can find wondrous forms of expression when they write to another. I've seen the thrilled reaction of a third-grader getting a reply from *Home Alone* star Macaulay Culkin after writing a fan letter. In cases like these, kids learn they can control their destiny in a world ruled by big people.

But what kind of letter should they write, and to whom? The answers are as varied as the children are. A letter can be a question or a complaint; a request or a declaration of love; a confession or a condemnation. The old axiom "kids are people, too" is undeniably true, and children comprise no less complex a constellation of feelings, opinions, hopes, and desires than do adults. Not only should we treat them accordingly, but we should encourage them to view themselves that way.

In the following pages, I have listed hundreds of celebrities, companies, institutions, officials, heroes, and villains, all of whom are of particular interest to children of varying ages. Kids who use this book will find that their voices matter, that those they write to will take a strong interest in what they have to say. Not every letter will get a personal response, but many will.

Since I published my first address book a number of years ago, I've been deluged with letters from individuals who found that by writing to an important legislator, reviled corporate villain, or favorite movie star, they had tapped into a unique source of power. They learned they were not isolated, and that they had the wherewithal to communicate *directly* with those who affected their lives. That can hold true for children as well.

Writing letters is purposeful work. Kids that normally rebel against rote learning drills will rise to the occasion when it comes to writing to their heroes, especially when they see that their letters are answered. Writing is a great habit to develop, and a hard habit to break.

My hope is that *The Kid's Address Book* will aid children in turning a corner. If they develop a love and appreciation for writing, for communicating, for interacting, and for taking action, then they'll be well on the way to becoming good citizens, caring adults, and builders of tomorrow's civilization. It all begins with a pen and a blank piece of paper.

—Michael Levine
Los Angeles

FAN MAIL

Your favorite actors, singers, entertainers, comic strip and cartoon characters, and sports figures.

Aaron, Chester
P.O. Box 388
Occidental, CA 95465

Author of Gideon *and* Hello to Bodega

Abbott, Jim
c/o California Angels
P.O. Box 2000
Anaheim, CA 92803

Professional baseball player

Abdul, Paula
30 West 21st Street
New York, NY 10010

Dancer/choreographer/singer

Adams, Bryan
1416 North La Brea Avenue
Hollywood, CA 90028

Singer

Adams, Richard George
26 Church Street
Whitchurch, Hampshire, England

Watership Down *author*

Aga Khan IV, H.H. Prince Karim
Aiglemont
60270 Gouvieux, France

Spiritual leader and Imam of Ismailian Muslims

Agassi, Andre
c/o Andre's Court Club
Dept. DA, P.O. Box 4297
Portland, OR 97208–4297

Professional tennis star/his fan club

Akihito
The Imperial Palace
1-1 Chiyoda-ku
Tokyo, Japan

Emperor of Japan

Allen, Woody
930 Fifth Avenue
New York, NY 10021

Director/writer/actor

Alley, Kirstie
10390 Santa Monica Boulevard,
Suite 310
Los Angeles, CA 90025
Actress, co-star of "Cheers"

Anderson, Harry
9830 Wilshire Boulevard
Beverly Hills, CA 90212
Actor/magician/comedian/co-star of "Night Court"

Anderson, O. J.
c/o New York Giants
Giants Stadium
East Rutherford, NJ 07073
Professional football player

Anderson, Richard Dean
R.R. 1 North
Jefferson, NH 03583
Actor, star of "MacGyver"

**Andre the Giant
(Roussimoff)**
P.O. Box 3859
Stamford, CT 06905
Professional wrestler

Andrews, V. C.
c/o Pocket Books
1230 Avenue of the Americas
New York, NY 10020
Author of Flowers in the Attic

Applegate, Christina
c/o "Married . . . With Children"
1438 North Gower Street
Los Angeles, CA 90028
Actress

**Arnold, Roseanne
(Barr)**
8436 West 3rd Street, #650
Los Angeles, CA 90048
Comedienne, actress

Austin, Tracy Ann
c/o Advantage International
1025 Thomas Jefferson, NW
Washington, DC 20007
Tennis player

Avi
c/o Orchard Press
Box 276
Shapleigh, ME 04076
. *Author of The True Confessions of Charlotte Doyle*

Badd, Johnny B.
P.O. Box 105366
Atlanta, GA 30348-5366
Professional wrestler

Baio, Scott
P.O. Box 5617
Beverly Hills, CA 90210
Actor

Barbie and Ken
5150 Rosecrans Avenue
Hawthorne, CA 90250
Famous doll and famous doll boyfriend

Barkley, Charles
c/o Philadelphia 76ers
P.O. Box 25040
Philadelphia, PA 19147
Professional basketball player

Barney and the Backyard Gang
Barney the Dinosaur
c/o Lyon's Group
300 East Bethany Road, P.O. Box 8000
Allen, TX 75002-1306

Popular video dinosaur

Bateman, Jason
P.O. Box 333
Woodland Hills, CA 91365

Actor

Bateman, Justine
3960 Laurel Canyon Boulevard, Suite 193
Studio City, CA 91604

Actress

Beach, "Sexy" Sonny
1692 Sprinter Street, NW
Atlanta, GA 30318

Professional wrestler

Beatty, Warren
1849 Sawtelle Avenue, #500
Los Angeles, CA 90069

Actor, star of Dick Tracy

Beauty and the Beast
c/o Disney Studios
500 South Buena Vista Street
Burbank, CA 91521

Cartoon heroine and her hero

Becker, Boris
Nusslocher Strasse 51, 6906 Leiman
Baden, Germany

Tennis star

Bentley, Ray
c/o Buffalo Bills
One Bills Drive
Orchard Park, NY 14127

Professional football player and author of children's books

Berenstain, Stan and Jan
c/o Random House Children's Books
225 Park Avenue South
New York, NY 10003

Authors of the Berenstain Bears series

Bergen, Candice
c/o Shukovsky/English
4000 Warner Boulevard
Burbank, CA 91522

Actress, star of "Murphy Brown"

Beverly Brothers
P.O. Box 3857
Stamford, CT 06905

Professional "tag team" wrestlers

Bialik, Mayim
c/o Booh Schut Agency
11350 Ventura Boulevard, Suite 206
Studio City, CA 91604

Actress, co-star of "Blossom"

Big Bird
c/o Children's Television Workshop
One Lincoln Plaza
New York, NY 10023

"Sesame Street" character

Bird, Larry
c/o Boston Celtics
150 Causeway Street
Boston, MA 02114
Professional basketball player

Blossom, Lady
P.O. Box 105366
Atlanta, GA 30348–5366
Professional wrestler

Blume, Judy
c/o Viking Penguin
375 Hudson Street
New York, NY 10014
Author, frequently voted as a favorite by kids nationwide

Boitano, Brian
c/o Leigh Steinberg
2737 Dunleer Place
Los Angeles, CA 90064
Ice skater, winner of 1988 Olympic Gold Medal

Bol, Manute
c/o Philadelphia 76ers
P.O. Box 25040
Philadelphia, PA 19147
Professional basketball player

Bolton, Michael
c/o Contemporary Communications
155 East 55th Street
New York, NY 10022
Pop singer

Bonet, Lisa
8322 Beverly Boulevard, Suite 202
Los Angeles, CA 90027
Actress

Bono, Steve
c/o San Francisco Giants
711 Nevada Street
Redwood City, CA 94061
Professional football player

Bosworth, Brian
c/o Seattle Seahawks
11220 Northeast 53rd Street
Kirkland, WA 98033
Football player

**Bozo the Clown
(Larry Harmon)**
5455 Wilshire Boulevard, Suite 2200
Los Angeles, CA 90036
Famous clown

Bradbury, Ray
c/o Bantam Books
666 Fifth Avenue
New York, NY 10103
Fantasy, science-fiction author

**The Brain
(Bobby Heenan)**
P.O. Box 3857
Stamford, CT 06905
Professional wrestler

Briggs, Joe Bob
P.O. Box 33
Dallas, TX 75221
Drive-in movie critic

Brokaw, Tom
c/o NBC News

30 Rockefeller Plaza
New York, NY 10112
Television journalist

Brooks, Garth
1750 North Vine Street
Hollywood, CA 90028
Singer

Brown, Charlie
One Snoopy Place
Santa Rosa, CA 95401
Much put-upon "Peanuts" character

Brown, Julie
c/o MTV
1515 Broadway, 23rd Floor
New York, NY 10036
Veejay

Bullwinkle, Rocky, Boris, Natasha, Dudley Do-Right, Snidely Whiplash, etc.
8218 Sunset Boulevard
Hollywood, CA 90046
Cartoon characters from the "Rocky and Bullwinkle Show"

The Bundys
(Al, Peg, Kelly, Bud, Buck)
10201 West Pico Boulevard
Los Angeles, CA 90035
"Married With Children" family

Bunny, Bugs
c/o Warner Brothers
4000 Warner Boulevard
Burbank, CA 91522
Famous cartoon bunny

Burke, Chris
c/o Abrams Artists & Associates
9200 Sunset Boulevard, Suite 625
Los Angeles, CA 90069
Actor, co-star of "Life Goes On"

Burton, LeVar
(Levardis Robert Martyn, Jr.)
9301 Wilshire Boulevard, Suite 312
Beverly Hills, CA 90210
Actor, co-star of "Star Trek: The Next Generation"

Bush, Barbara Pierce
The White House
1600 Pennsylvania Avenue
Washington, DC 20500
First Lady of the United States

Bushwackers, The
(Butch and Luke)
P.O. Box 3857
Stamford, CT 06905
Professional "tag team" wrestlers

California Raisins
c/o Will Vinton
1400 NW 22nd Avenue
Portland, OR 97210
Dancing raisins

Call, Brandon
9744 Wilshire Boulevard, Suite 206
Beverly Hills, CA 90212
Actor

Cameron, Kirk
9560 Wilshire Boulevard, Suite 500
Beverly Hills, CA 90212
Actor, co-star of "Growing Pains"

Candy, John
8899 Beverly Boulevard
Los Angeles, CA 90048
Comic actor

Canseco, José
c/o California Angels
P.O. Box 2000
Anaheim, CA 92803
Professional baseball player

Capriati, Jennifer
c/o International Management Group
One Erieview Plaza, Suite 1300
Cleveland, OH 44114
Young professional tennis player

Carey, Mariah
51 West 52nd Street
New York, NY 10019
Singer

Carle, Eric
c/o Philomel Books
200 Madison Avenue
New York, NY 10016
Author of 1991 best-seller The Very Quiet Cricket

Carpenter, John
8383 Wilshire Boulevard, Suite 840
Beverly Hills, CA 90211
Horror/suspense film director

Carteris, Gabrielle
8428 Melrose Place, Suite B
Los Angeles, CA 90069
Actress, co-star of "Beverly Hills 90210"

Carvey, Dana
30 Rockefeller Plaza, Suite 1700
New York, NY 10019
Comedian, co-star of "Saturday Night Live"

Chambers, Tom
c/o Phoenix Suns
P.O. Box 1369
Phoenix, AZ 85001
Professional basketball player

Chapman, Tracy
c/o Lookout
506 Santa Monica Boulevard
Santa Monica, CA 90401
Singer/songwriter

Chlumsky, Anna
10100 Santa Monica Boulevard, 16th Floor
Los Angeles, CA 90067
Actress, star of My Girl

Church Lady, The
c/o "Saturday Night Live"
30 Rockefeller Plaza
New York, NY 10112
Hostess of "Church Chat"

Claus, Santa
(also Mrs. Claus, Elves, Dancer, Prancer, Donder, Vixen, Cupid, Rudolph, Dasher, Comet, and Blitzen)
North Pole 30351

Cleary, Beverly Atlee
c/o William Morrow and Company
1350 Avenue of the Americas
New York, NY 10020

Popular author of books for children and teenagers

Cliff, Jimmy
c/o Victor Chambers
51 Lady Musgrave Road
Kingston, Jamaica

Reggae singer

Cole, Joanna
c/o Scholastic Inc.
730 Broadway
New York, NY 10003

Author

Cole, Natalie
1750 North Vine Street
Hollywood, CA 90028

Singer

Collins, Phil
Shalford
Surrey, England

Rock musician

Connors, Jimmy
c/o ProServ
888 17th Street, NW
Washington, DC 20006

Tennis player

Copperfield, David
9107 Wilshire Boulevard, Suite 500
Beverly Hills, CA 90210

Magician

Cornelius, Don
9255 Sunset Boulevard, Suite 420
Los Angeles, CA 90039

Host of "Soul Train"

Cosby, Bill
P.O. Box 808
Greenfield, MA 01301

Actor/comedian

Costner, Kevin
151 El Camino Drive
Beverly Hills, CA 90212

Actor

Craven, Wes
c/o Henri Bollinger
9200 Sunset Boulevard, Suite 418
Los Angeles, CA 90048

Horror-film director

Cruise, Tom
(Thomas Cruise Mapother IV)
9830 Wilshire Boulevard
Beverly Hills, CA 90212

Actor

Cryer, Jon
10000 West Washington Boulevard, Suite 3018
Culver City, CA 90232

Actor

Crystal, Billy
c/o Rollins
801 Westmount Drive
Los Angeles, CA 90069
Comedian

Culkin, Macaulay
8899 Beverly Boulevard
Los Angeles, CA 90048
Actor, star of Home Alone

Curry, Adam
c/o MTV
1515 Broadway, 23rd Floor
New York, NY 10036
MTV video countdown veejay

D. J. Jazzy Jeff
(Jeff Townes)
1133 Avenue of the Americas
New York, NY 10036
Singer

Dailey, Janet
P.O. Box 2197
Branson, MO 65616
Author

Dalton, Timothy
c/o James Sharkey
15 Golden Square
London W1 England
Actor, current James Bond

Danson, Ted
9830 Wilshire Boulevard
Beverly Hills, CA 90212
Actor, co-star of "Cheers"

Danza, Tony
8899 Beverly Boulevard
Los Angeles, CA 90048
Actor, co-star of "Who's the Boss?"

Davis, Jim
(James Robert)
c/o United Features Syndicate
200 Park Avenue
New York, NY 10166
Cartoonist, creator of "Garfield"

DeBarge, El
6255 Sunset Boulevard, Suite 624
Los Angeles, CA 90028
Singer

Deighton, Len
Fairymount, Blackrock, Dundalk
County Louth, Ireland
Author

DeLuise, Peter
151 El Camino Drive
Beverly Hills, CA 90212
Actor, co-star of "21 Jump Street"

Dempsey, Patrick
10100 Santa Monica Boulevard, Suite 1600
Los Angeles, CA 90067
Actor

Depp, Johnny
1901 Avenue of the Stars, Suite 840
Los Angeles, CA 90067
Actor

Dern, Laura
760 North La Cienega Boulevard
Los Angeles, CA 90069
Actress

DesBarres, Michael
P.O. Box 4160
Hollywood, CA 90078
Singer/actor

DeVito, Danny
P.O. Box 27365
Los Angeles, CA 90027
Actor/director

Doherty, Shannen
2525 Sunset Boulevard, 6th
 Floor
Los Angeles, CA 90028
*Actress, co-star of "Beverly Hills
90210"*

Donahue, Phil
300 Central Park West
New York, NY 10024
Talk show host

Downey, Robert Jr.
9830 Wilshire Boulevard
Beverly Hills, CA 90212
Actor

Drucker, Mort
c/o MAD Magazine
485 Madison Avenue
New York, NY 10022
Cartoonist

Dumars, Joe
c/o Detroit Pistons
One Championship Drive
Auburn Hills, MI 48057
Professional basketball player

Ebert, Roger
c/o New York *Daily News*
220 East 42nd Street
New York, NY 10017
Film critic

Eggert, Nicole
c/o William Carroll Agency
120 South Victory Boulevard,
 Suite 502
Burbank, CA 91502
Actress

**Enforcers, The
(Arn Anderson and Larry
Zbyszko)**
P.O. Box 105366
Atlanta, GA 30348–5366
*Professional "tag team"
wrestlers*

Englund, Robert
9200 Sunset Boulevard, Suite
 625
Los Angeles, CA 90069
*Actor, portrays "Freddy
Krueger"*

Esiason, Norman (Boomer)
c/o Cincinnati Bengals
200 Riverfront Stadium
Cincinnati, OH 45202
Professional football player

**Ferguson, Sarah Margaret
(Windsor)**
Buckingham Palace
London SW1 England
"Fergie," Duchess of York

Fleisher, Charles
c/o Walt Disney Pictures
500 South Buena Vista Street
Burbank, CA 91521
Actor/comedian/voice of Roger Rabbit

**The Flintstones
(Fred, Wilma, Pebbles, Dino)**
3400 Cahuenga Boulevard, West
Hollywood, CA 90068
Cartoon family

Ford, Harrison
P.O. Box 5617
Beverly Hills, CA 90210
Actor

**Foster, Jodie
(Alicia Christian)**
8899 Beverly Boulevard
Los Angeles, CA 90048
Actress/director

Fox, Michael J.
9560 Wilshire Boulevard, Suite 500
Beverly Hills, CA 90212
Actor

Frasier, Debra
c/o Harcourt, Brace, Jovanovich
Children's Book Division
1250 Sixth Avenue
San Diego, CA 92101
Author

**Fresh Prince
(Will Smith)**
1133 Avenue of the Americas
New York, NY 10036
Singer/actor/star of "Fresh Prince of Bel Air"

Frye, Soleil Moon
1801 Avenue of the Stars, Suite 1250
Los Angeles, CA 90067
Actress, still seen as star of "Punky Brewster" in syndication

Gabriel, Peter
25 Ives Street
London SW3 England
Singer

Garth, Jennie
12725 Ventura Boulevard, Suite E
Studio City, CA 91604
Actress, co-star of "Beverly Hills 90210"

Gibson, Debbie
P.O. Box 489
Merrick, NY 11566
Singer/songwriter

Gibson, Mel
P.O. Box 2156
Santa Monica, CA 90406
Actor

Gilbert, Sara
10100 Santa Monica Boulevard, 16th Floor
Los Angeles, CA 90067
Actress, co-star of "Roseanne"

**Godden, Rumer
(Margaret)**
Ardnacloich, Moniaive, Thornhill
Dumfriesshire D63 4HZ
Scotland
Author

Gold, Tracey
12725 Ventura Boulevard,
   Suite E
Studio City, CA 91604
*Actress, co-star of "Growing
Pains"*

**Goldberg, Whoopi
(Caryn Johnson)**
9830 Wilshire Boulevard
Beverly Hills, CA 90212
Actress/comedienne

Goodman, John
P.O. Box 5617
Beverly Hills, CA 90210
Actor, co-star of "Roseanne"

Gorbachev, Mikhail Sergeyevich
Staraya pl 4
Moscow, Russia
Former president of the USSR

Gosselaar, Mark Paul
261 South Robertson Boulevard
Beverly Hills, CA 90211
*Actor, co-star of "Saved by the
Bell"*

**Graf, Steffi
(Stephanie Maria)**
12-D 6000 Frankfurt-am-Main
71, Germany
Tennis player

Grant, Amy
Riverstone Farm, Moran Road
Franklin, TN 37064
Singer

Green, A. C.
c/o LA Lakers
P.O. Box 10
Inglewood, CA 90306
Basketball player

Green, Brian Austin
7813 Sunset Boulevard
Los Angeles, CA 90046
*Actor, co-star of "Beverly Hills
90210"*

Gretzky, Wayne
c/o Los Angeles Kings
P.O. Box 17013
Inglewood, CA 90308
Hockey player

Grey, Jennifer
121 North San Vicente Boulevard
Beverly Hills, CA 90211
Actress

Grieco, Richard
9830 Wilshire Boulevard
Beverly Hills, CA 90212
Actor

Griffith, Melanie
8899 Beverly Boulevard
Los Angeles, CA 90048
Actress

Groening, Matt
10201 West Pico Boulevard
Los Angeles, CA 90035
"Simpsons" cartoonist

Guisewite, Cathy Lee
c/o Universal Press Syndicate
4900 Main Street
Kansas City, MO 64112
"Cathy" cartoonist

Guy, Jasmine
14755 Ventura Boulevard,
    #1-710
Sherman Oaks, CA 91403
Actress/singer/dancer/co-star of "A Different World"

Haim, Corey
9000 Sunset Boulevard, Suite
    1200
Los Angeles, CA 90069
Actor

Hall, Arsenio
c/o Paramount Television
5555 Melrose Avenue
Hollywood, CA 90038
Talk show host

**Hammer
(formerly M. C.)**
1750 North Vine Street
Hollywood, CA 90028
Rapper

**The Hammer
(Greg Valentine)**
P.O. Box 3857
Stamford, CT 06905
Professional wrestler

Handford, Martin
c/o Little, Brown and Company
34 Beacon Street
Boston, MA 02108
Where's Waldo author

Hanks, Tom
P.O. Box 1278
Los Angeles, CA 90049
Actor

Harris, Neil Patrick
11350 Ventura Boulevard, Suite
    206
Studio City, CA 91604
Actor, star of "Doogie Howser, M.D."

Hart, Mary
c/o "Entertainment Tonight"
5555 Melrose Avenue
Hollywood, CA 90038
Host of entertainment news magazine show

Henderson, Rickey
c/o Oakland Athletics
Oakland-Alameda County
    Stadium
Oakland, CA 94621
Professional baseball player

Henning, Doug
11940 San Vicente Boulevard,
    Suite 49032
Los Angeles, CA 90049
Magician

**Herman, Pee-Wee
(Paul Reubens)**
P.O. Box 48243

Los Angeles, CA 90048

Comic actor

Hervey, Jason
c/o Abrams Artists and
   Associates
9200 Sunset Boulevard, Suite
   625
Los Angeles, CA 90069

Actor, co-star of "The Wonder Years"

Hewitt, Love
1901 Avenue of the Stars, 16th
   Floor
Los Angeles, CA 90067

Singer, actress, co-star of "Kid's Inc."

**Hinton, S. E.
(Susan Eloise)**
8955 Beverly Boulevard
Los Angeles, CA 90048

Author

**Hit Man, The
(Brett Hart)**
P.O. Box 3857
Stamford, CT 06905

Professional wrestler

Hoffman, Dustin
9830 Wilshire Boulevard
Beverly Hills, CA 90212

Actor

**Hogan, Hulk
(Terry Gene Bollea)**
P.O. Box 3859
Stamford, CT 06905

Professional wrestling champion

**Holt, Victoria
(Eleanor Alice Burford Hibbert)**
c/o A. M. Heath
40 William IV Street
London WC2N 4DD
England

Romance novelist

Houston, Whitney
410 East 50th Street
New York, NY 10022

Singer

Howard, Desmond
c/o Michigan State University
Athletic Department
East Lansing, MI 48824

1991 Heisman Trophy Winner. Received more votes than any other recipient

Hudson, Eleanor
c/o Random House Children's
   Books
225 Park Avenue South
New York, NY 10003

Author of Teenage Mutant Ninja Turtles' Pizza Party

Hughes, John
100 Universal City Plaza, Suite
   507
Universal City, CA 91608

Film writer/producer/director

Hyatt, Missy
P.O. Box 105366
Atlanta, GA 30348–5366

Professional wrestler

Ice-T
c/o Sire Records
75 Rockefeller Plaza
New York, NY 10019
Rap singer

Jackson, Bo (Vincent)
P.O. Box 2517
Auburn, AL 36831
Athlete

Jackson, Janet
1416 North La Brea Avenue
Hollywood, CA 90028
Singer

Jackson, Reverend Jesse Louis
930 East 50th Street
Chicago, IL 60615
Politician, civil rights leader

Jackson, Michael
1801 Century Park West
Los Angeles, CA 90067
Singer

Jeffers, Susan
c/o Dial Books for Young Readers
375 Hudson Street
New York, NY 10014
Illustrator of Brother Eagle,
Sister Sky

Jennings, Stanford
c/o Cincinnati Bengals
200 Riverfront Stadium
Cincinnati, OH 45202
Professional football player

The Jetsons
(George, Jane, Judy, Elroy, and
Astro)
3400 Cahuenga Boulevard, West
Hollywood, CA 90069
Space-age cartoon family

Johnson, Earvin "Magic"
c/o First Team Marketing
1801 Avenue of the Stars
Los Angeles, CA 90067
Former Lakers basketball star,
fund-raiser for various charities,
and HIV spokesperson. Mem-
ber of the National Commission
on Aids

Johnson, Kevin
c/o Phoenix Suns
P.O. Box 1369
Phoenix, AZ 85001
Professional basketball player

Jordan, Michael
c/o Chicago Bulls
980 North Michigan Avenue,
  Suite 1600
Chicago, IL 60611
Professional basketball player

Justice, Sid
P.O. Box 3857
Stamford, CT 06905
Professional wrestler

Karoly, Bela
c/o Karoly's Gymnastics
17203 Bamwood
Houston, TX 77090
Gymnastic coach

Katz, Omri
12725 Ventura Boulevard,
   Suite E
Studio City, CA 91604
Actor

Kemp, Shawn
c/o Seattle Supersonics
C-Box 900911
Seattle, WA 98109
Professional basketball player

**Kenny G
(Gorelick)**
648 North Robertson Boulevard
Los Angeles, CA 90048
Saxophonist

King, Stephen
c/o Viking Penguin
375 Hudson Street
New York, NY 10014
Author

Lambeer, Bill
c/o Detroit Pistons
One Championship Drive
Auburn Hills, MI 48057
Professional basketball player

Lang, K. D.
41 Britain Street, Suite 200
Toronto, Ontario M5A 1R7
   Canada
Singer

Larkin, Barry
c/o Cincinnati Reds
100 Riverfront Stadium
Cincinnati, OH 45202
Professional baseball player

Leach, Robin
c/o TPE
1014 North Sycamore
Los Angeles, CA 90038
*"Lifestyles of the Rich and
Famous" host*

Legion of Doom
P.O. Box 3857
Stamford, CT 06905
*Professional "tag team"
wrestlers*

LeMond, Greg
c/o ProServ
1101 Wilson Boulevard, Suite
   1800
Arlington, VA 22209
Champion bicyclist

Leno, Jay
9000 Sunset Boulevard, Suite
   400
Los Angeles, CA 90069
"Tonight Show" host

Letterman, David
30 Rockefeller Plaza, Suite 1400
New York, NY 10020
"Late Night" host

Levine, Michael
8730 Sunset Boulevard, 6th
   Floor
Los Angeles, CA 90069
Author, Kid's Address Book

Little Mermaid, The
c/o Disney Studios
500 South Buena Vista Street
Burbank, CA 91521
Cartoon heroine

LL Cool J
(Ladies Love Cool James)
298 Elizabeth Street
New York, NY 10012
Rap singer

Lloyd, Christopher
222 North Canyon Drive, Suite 202
Beverly Hills, CA 90210
Actor

Luger, Lex
P.O. Box 105366
Atlanta, GA 30348–5366
Professional wrestler

Lundgren, Dolph
1875 Century Park East, Suite 2200
Los Angeles, CA 90067
Actor

Macho Man
(Randy Savage)
P.O. Box 3857
Stamford, CT 06905
Professional wrestler

Madonna
(Madonna Louise Ciccone)
9200 Sunset Boulevard, Suite 915
Los Angeles, CA 90069
Singer/actress/songwriter

Malone, Karl "The Mailman"
c/o Utah Jazz
5 Triad Center
Salt Lake City, UT 84180
Professional basketball player

Marky Mark
(Mark Wahlberg)
10900 Wilshire Boulevard
Los Angeles, CA 90024
Rap singer

Martin, Ann M.
c/o Scholastic, Inc.
730 Broadway
New York, NY 10022
Author of the Baby Sitter books

Martin, Kellie
6212 Banner Avenue
Hollywood, CA 90038
Actress, co-star of "Life Goes On"

Marx, Richard
1750 North Vine Street
Hollywood, CA 90028
Singer

Mattingly, Don
c/o New York Yankees
Yankee Stadium
Bronx, NY 10451
Professional baseball player

McDonald, Ronald
One McDonald Plaza
Oak Brook, IL 60521
Spokesclown and fund-raiser for children's hospitals

McDowell, Jack
c/o Chicago White Sox
324 West 35th Street
Chicago, IL 60616

Professional baseball player and musician

McEntire, Reba
1514 South Street
Nashville, TN 37212

Singer

McHale, Kevin
c/o Boston Celtics
150 Causeway Street
Boston, MA 02114

Professional basketball player

McKellar, Danica
6212 Banner Avenue
Hollywood, CA 90038

Actress

Mellen, Brian
c/o New York Rangers
Four Penn Plaza
New York, NY 10001

Professional hockey player

**Mellencamp, John
(formerly Cougar)**
825 Eighth Avenue
New York, NY 10019

Singer

Milano, Alyssa
P.O. Box 3684
Hollywood, CA 90078

Actress, co-star of "Who's the Boss?"

Miller, Reggie
c/o Indiana Pacers
300 East Market Street
Indianapolis, IN 46204

Professional basketball player and teen talk show host

Montana, Joe
c/o San Francisco 49ers
711 Nevada Street
Redwood City, NV 94061

Professional football player

Moon, Warren
c/o Houston Oilers
6910 Funnin Street
Houston, TX 77030

Professional football player

Morris, Jack
c/o Minnesota Twins
501 Chicago Avenue, South
Minneapolis, MN 55415

Baseball pitcher, 1991 World Series Most Valuable Player

Mousekowitz, Fievel
c/o Amblin Entertainment
100 Universal City Plaza
Universal City, CA 91609

Cartoon mouse

**Mr. Rogers
(Fred)**
c/o Family Communications
4802 Fifth Avenue
Pittsburgh, PA 15213

Kids' program host

Mr. Wizard
(Donald Jeffrey Herbert)
P.O. Box 83
Canoga Park, CA 91305
Television science teacher

Ms. Elizabeth
P.O. Box 3857
Stamford, CT 06905
Professional wrestler

Mullin, Chris
c/o Golden State Warriors
Nimitz Freeway and Hegen-
berger Road
Oakland, CA 94621
Professional basketball player

Murphy, Eddie
5555 Melrose Avenue
Los Angeles, CA 90038
Actor/comedian/producer

Nasty Boys, The
P.O. Box 3857
Stamford, CT 06905
Professional "tag team"
wrestlers

Natural Disasters
(The Earthquake and Tycoon)
P.O. Box 3857
Stamford, CT 06905
Professional "tag team"
wrestlers

Navratilova, Martina
c/o International Management
Group
One Erieview Plaza
Cleveland, OH 44114
Tennis player

Norman the Lunatic
(Makhan Singh)
1692 Sprinter Street, NW
Atlanta, GA 30318
Professional wrestler

O'Connor, Sinead
13 Red Lion Square, 10 Halsey
House
London WC1 England
Singer

Okino, Betty
c/o Karoly's Gymnastics
17203 Bamwood
Houston, TX 77090
Gymnast

Olsen, Ashley and Mary Kate
c/o Robert Thorne
10100 Santa Monica Boulevard,
Suite 2200
Los Angeles, CA 90067
Twins who play one character
on "Full House"

Osbourne, Ozzy
1801 Century Park West
Los Angeles, CA 90067
Singer

Parish, Robert
c/o Boston Celtics
150 Causeway Street
Boston, MA 02114
Professional basketball player

Pat
c/o "Saturday Night Live"
30 Rockefeller Plaza
New York, NY 10112
Androgynous whiner

Pelham, David
c/o Dutton Children's Books
375 Hudson Street
New York, NY 10014
Author of Sam's Sandwich

Perry, Luke
1801 Avenue of the Stars, Suite
   1250
Los Angeles, CA 90067
*Actor, co-star of "Beverly Hills
90210"*

Phoenix, River
P.O. Box 520
Royal Palm Beach, FL 33411
Actor

Pike, Christopher
c/o Pocket/Archway
1230 Avenue of the Americas
New York, NY 10020
Author

Pippen, Scottie
c/o Chicago Bulls
980 North Michigan Avenue
Chicago, IL 60611
Professional basketball player

Porter, Alisan
c/o InterTalent
131 South Rodeo Drive, Suite
   300
Beverly Hills, CA 90212
Actress, co-star of Curly Sue

Prelutsky, Jack
c/o Alfred A. Knopf, Inc.
201 East 50th Street
New York, NY 10022
Author

Priestley, Jason
2121 Avenue of the Stars, Suite
   950
Los Angeles, CA 90067
*Actor, co-star of "Beverly Hills
90210"*

Prince
3300 Warner Boulevard
Burbank, CA 91510
Singer

**Princess Diana
(Spencer Windsor)**
Kensington Palace
London W8 England
Princess "Di," Princess of Wales

Puett, Tommy
9000 Sunset Boulevard, Suite
   1200
Los Angeles, CA 90069
Actor, co-star of "Life Goes On"

**Queen Beatrix
(Wilhelmina Armagard)**
Binnen Huf 19
The Hague 2513 AA, The
   Netherlands
Queen of The Netherlands

Quinn, Martha
c/o MTV
1515 Broadway
New York, NY 10019
MTV hostess

Rabbit, Roger
c/o Touchstone Pictures
500 South Buena Vista Street
Burbank, CA 91521
Cartoon rabbit

Raffi
(Cavoukian)
c/o Jensen Communications
120 South Victory Boulevard,
   Suite 201
Burbank, CA 91502
Singer

Raitt, Bonnie
1750 North Vine Street
Hollywood, CA 90028
Singer

Randall, Ethan
261 South Robertson Boulevard
Beverly Hills, CA 90211
Actor

Raphael, Sally Jesse
510 West 57th Street
New York, NY 10019
Talk show host

Reeves, Keanu
9100 Sunset Boulevard, Suite
   300
Los Angeles, CA 90069
Actor

Renegade Warriors, The
(Chris and Mark Youngblood)
1692 Sprinter Street, NW
Atlanta, GA 30318
Professional "tag-team"
wrestlers

Richmond, Mitch
c/o Golden State Warriors
The Oakland Coliseum Arena
Oakland, CA 94621
Professional basketball player

Roberts, Julia
8899 Beverly Boulevard
Los Angeles, CA 90048
Actress

Roman, Larry
c/o "Saturday Night Live"
30 Rockefeller Plaza
New York, NY 10112
News commentator

Ryder, Winona
(Horowitz)
8899 Beverly Boulevard
Los Angeles, CA 90048
Actress

Saget, Bob
8899 Beverly Boulevard
Los Angeles, CA 90048
Actor/comedian/TV host

Sanders, Barry
c/o Detroit Lions
P.O. Box 4200
Pontiac, MI 48057
Professional football player

Savage, Fred
1450 Belfast Drive
Los Angeles, CA 90069
Actor, star of "The Wonder Years"

Schulz, Charles Monroe
One Snoopy Place
Santa Rosa, CA 95401
"Peanuts" cartoonist

Schwarzenegger, Arnold
c/o Oak Productions
321 Hampton Drive, Suite 20
Venice, CA 90291
Actor/Special Olympics trainer

Schwarzkopf, Norman H.
c/o ICM
8899 Beverly Boulevard
Los Angeles, CA 90048
Retired Army general, hero of Desert Storm

Scieszka, Jon
c/o Viking Press
375 Hudson Street
New York, NY 10014
Author

Scott, Byron
c/o Los Angeles Lakers
P.O. Box 10
Inglewood, CA 90306
Professional basketball player

Seles, Monica
c/o International Management
  Group
One Erieview Plaza, Suite 1300
Cleveland, OH 44114

Professional tennis player

Sendak, Maurice Bernard
c/o HarperCollins
10 East 53rd Street
New York, NY 10022
Children's book illustrator/author

Sgt. Slaughter
P.O. Box 3857
Stamford, CT 06905
Professional wrestler

Short, Martin
9830 Wilshire Boulevard
Beverly Hills, CA 90212
Actor/comedian

**Simpsons, The
(Homer, Marge, Lisa, Maggie, and Bart)**
10201 West Pico Boulevard
Los Angeles, CA 90035
Cartoon family

Slater, Christian
9830 Wilshire Boulevard
Beverly Hills, CA 90212
Actor

Smiley, John
c/o Pittsburgh Pirates
600 Stadium Circle
Pittsburgh, PA 15212
Professional baseball player

Spelling, Tori
1450 Belfast Drive
Los Angeles, CA 90069
Actress, co-star of "Beverly Hills 90210"

Spielberg, Steven
c/o Amblin Entertainment
100 Universal City Plaza, Suite
   477
Universal City, CA 91608
Film director/producer

Spinelli, Jerry
c/o Little, Brown and Company
34 Beacon Street
Boston, MA 02108
Author of Maniac Magee, *1991
Newbery Award Winner*

Stamos, John
151 El Camino Drive
Beverly Hills, CA 90212
Actor, co-star of "Full House"

Strawberry, Darryl
c/o Los Angeles Dodgers
1000 Elysian Park Avenue
Los Angeles, CA 90012
Professional baseball player

Studd, Diamond
P.O. Box 105366
Atlanta, GA 30348–5366
Professional wrestler

**Super Dave
(Bob Einstein)**
8955 Beverly Boulevard
Los Angeles, CA 90048
Comic stuntman

Sutherland, Kiefer
9200 Sunset Boulevard, Suite 25
Los Angeles, CA 90069
Actor

Swayze, Patrick
8436 West Third Street, Suite
   650
Los Angeles, CA 90048
Actor/dancer

Sweetin, Jodie
6212 Banner Avenue
Hollywood, CA 90038
Actress, co-star of "Full House"

Taylor, Lawrence
c/o New York Giants
Giants Stadium
East Rutherford, NJ 07073
Professional football player

Teenage Mutant Ninja Turtles
c/o New Line Cinema
116 North Robertson Boulevard,
   Suite 200
Los Angeles, CA 90048
*Michelangelo, Donatello,
Leonardo, and Raphael, super-
heroes on a half shell*

Thomas, Derrick
c/o Kansas City Chiefs
One Arrowhead Drive
Kansas City, MO 64129
Professional football player

Thomas, Isiah
c/o Detroit Pistons
Two Championship Drive
Auburn Hills, MI 48326
Professional basketball player

Tony the Tiger
c/o Kellogg Company
235 Porter
Battle Creek, MI 49017
Kellogg's mascot

Tyson, Mike
9 West 57th Street, Suite 4800
New York, NY 10019
Boxer

Ultimate Warrior
P.O. Box 3857
Stamford, CT 06905
Professional wrestler

Van Damme, Jean-Claude
P.O. Box 69A05
Los Angeles, CA 90069
Actor/martial arts expert

Vanilla Ice
8730 Sunset Boulevard, 5th
    Floor West
Los Angeles, CA 90069
Singer

Vincent, Francis T., Jr.
Commissioner's Office
350 Park Avenue
New York, NY 10022
Commissioner of baseball

Walker, Alice Malsenior
c/o Harcourt Brace Jovanovich
111 Fifth Avenue
New York, NY 10003
Author

Walters, Barbara
c/o ABC News
1330 Sixth Avenue
New York, NY 10019
Television journalist, co-host of "20/20"

Warlord
P.O. Box 3857
Stamford, CT 06905
Professional wrestler

Warner, Malcolm Jamal
c/o Artists First
8230 Beverly Boulevard,
    Suite 23
Los Angeles, CA 90048
Actor, co-star of "The Cosby Show"

Wayans, Keenen Ivory
P.O. Box 900
Beverly Hills, CA 90213
Executive producer and star of "In Living Color"

White, Jaleel
1450 Belfast Drive
Los Angeles, CA 90069
Actor, co-star of "Family Matters"

**Wild Thing
(Stevie Ray)**
1692 Sprinter Street, NW
Atlanta, GA 30318
Professional wrestler

Willis, Bruce
10100 Santa Monica Boulevard,
   Suite 1600
Los Angeles, CA 90067

Actor

Winfrey, Oprah
c/o Harpo Productions
35 East Wacker Street, Suite
   1782
Chicago, IL 60601

*Talk show host/children's
activist*

Worthy, James
c/o LA Lakers
P.O. Box 10
Inglewood, CA 90306

Basketball player

Young, Steve
c/o San Francisco 49ers
4949 Centennial Boulevard
Santa Clara, CA 95054–1229

Professional football player

Ziering, Ian
335 North Maple Drive,
   Suite 360
Beverly Hills, CA 90210

*Actor, co-star of "Beverly Hills
90210"*

Zmeskal, Kim
c/o Karoly's Gymnastics
17203 Bamwood
Houston, TX 77090

Gymnast

MUSIC MAKERS

Record companies and singing groups. Individual singers and entertainers are listed in section 1, Fan Mail.

A & M Records, Inc.
1416 North La Brea Avenue
Hollywood, CA 90028
Herb Alpert, chairman

Record company

AC/DC
11 Leonminster Road, Morden
Surrey SM4 England

Rock band

Aerosmith
c/o Fan Club
P.O. Box 4668
San Francisco, CA 94101

Rock group

Apollo Theatre Records, Inc., a subsidiary of Motown Record Co.
60 East 42nd Street, Suite 1334
New York, NY 10017
Jheryl Busby, president/CEO

Record company

Arista Records, Inc.
6 West 57th Street
New York, NY 10019

Clive Davis, president

Record company

Atlantic Records
75 Rockefeller Plaza
New York, NY 10019
Ahmet M. Ertegun, chairman/ CEO

Record company

Beastie Boys, The
1750 North Vine Street
Hollywood, CA 90028

Rap group

BMG
1133 Avenue of the Americas
New York, NY 10036
Michael Dornemann, chairman/ CEO

Record company

Bon Jovi
c/o Fan Club
P.O. Box 4843
San Francisco, CA 94101

Rock group

Boyz II Men
729 Seventh Avenue, 12th Floor
New York, NY 10019

Singing group

Capitol Records, Inc.
1750 North Vine Street
Hollywood, CA 90028
Jim Fifield, CEO

Record company

Caroline Records, Inc.
114 West 26th Street, 11th Floor
New York, NY 10001
Keith Wood, president

Record company

CBS Records Inc.
51 West 52nd Street
New York, NY 10019
Walter Yetnikoff, president & CEO

Record company

Chrysalis Records, Inc.
9255 Sunset Boulevard, Suite
319
Los Angeles, CA 90069
John Sykes, president

Recording company

Color Me Badd
c/o Reprise Records
3300 Warner Boulevard
Burbank, CA 91505

Singing group

**Columbia Records,
a division of CBS/Records
Group**
51 West 52nd Street
New York, NY 10019

Don Ienner, president

Recording company

Curb Records
3907 West Alameda Avenue, 2nd
Floor
Burbank, CA 91505
Mike Curb, chairman/president

Recording company

Def Leppard
P.O. Box 670
Old Chelsea Station
New York, NY 10113

Hard-rock band

**Elektra Entertainment,
a division of Warner Communications**
345 North Maple Drive, Suite
123
Beverly Hills, CA 90210
Bob Krasnow, chairman

Record label

**EMF
Mark Decloedt, James Atkin,
Zac Foley, Ian Dench, Derry
Brownson**
810 Seventh Avenue
New York, NY 10022

Punk-rock group

**EMI
a division of Capitol-EMI
Music, Inc.**
1800 North Vine Street
Hollywood, CA 90028
Jim Fifield, CEO

Record label

Enigma Records
136 West 18th Street, 2nd Floor
New York, NY 10011
William Hein, president

Recording company

Epic Records
1801 Century Park West
Los Angeles, CA 90067
Glen Brunman, VP Media and
   Artist Development

Record label

**Eurythmics
(Annie Lennox/Dave Stewart)**
P.O. Box 245
London N8 90G England

Rock musicians

Fat Boys, The
250 West 57th Street, Suite 1723
New York, NY 10107

Rap group

Geffen Records
9130 Sunset Boulevard
Los Angeles, CA 90069
David Geffen, chairman

Record label

Genesis
25 Ives Street
London SW3 England

Rock band

**Gloria Estefan and the Miami
Sound Machine**
8390 S.W. 4th Street
Miami, FL 33144

Pop group

Grateful Dead, The
P.O. Box 1566, Main Office Street
Montclair, NJ 07043

Cult rock band

**Great Jones,
a subsidiary of Island Records**
14 East 4th Street
New York, NY 10012
Mike Bone, president

Record label

Great White
P.O. Box 67487
Los Angeles, CA 90067

Rock band

Guns N' Roses
9130 Sunset Boulevard
Los Angeles, CA 90069

Heavy-metal group

**I.R.S.
International Record Syndicate,
Inc.**
3939 Lakershim Boulevard
Universal City, CA 91604
Miles Copeland, chairman

Recording company

**La's
Lee Mavers, Neil Mavers,
Cammy Power, John Power**
825 Eighth Avenue
New York, NY 10022

Musical group from England

**MCA Records/MCA Music
Entertainment Group**
1755 Broadway, 8th Floor
New York, NY 10019

Al Teller, chairman

Record label

Metallica
75 Rockefeller Plaza
New York, NY 10019

Rock group

Motley Crüe
345 North Maple Drive, Suite
123
Beverly Hills, CA 90210

Rock group

Motown Record Company, L.P.
729 Seventh Avenue, 12th Floor
New York, NY 10019
Jheryl Busby, president/CEO

Recording company

Naughty by Nature
c/o Tommy Boy Records
1747 First Avenue
New York, NY 10128

Singing group

**Nelson
(Matt and Gunnar)**
9130 Sunset Boulevard
Los Angeles, CA 90069

*Singing duo, third generation of
musical Nelsons*

New Kids on the Block
Six St. Gregory Street, Suite 7001
Dorchester, MA 02124

Pop group

Nirvana
9130 Sunset Boulevard
Los Angeles, CA 90069

Rock group

The Party
P.O. Box 2510
Los Angeles, CA 90078

Pop group

**P C Quest
Drew Nichols, Kim Whipkey,
Steve Petree, Chad Petree**
1133 Avenue of the Americas
New York, NY 10036

Singing group

P M Dawn
14 East 4th Street
New York, NY 10012

Rock group

Poison
1750 North Vine Street
Hollywood, CA 90028

Rock group

Polygram Records, Inc.
3800 West Alameda Avenue,
Suite 1500
Burbank, CA 91505
Peter Takiff, executive vice-
president, Administration

Recording company

Public Enemy
c/o Columbia Records
1801 Century Park West
Los Angeles, CA 90067

Rock group

**RCA Records,
a division of BMG Music**
1133 Avenue of the Americas
New York, NY 10036

Joe Galante, president

Recording company

R.E.M.
P.O. Box 8032
Athens, GA 30603

Rock band

Roxette
Marie Fredrikson, Per Gessle
1800 North Vine Street
Hollywood, CA 90028

Singing duo from Sweden

Skid Row
9229 Sunset Boulevard, Suite 710
Los Angeles, CA 90069–2474

Rock group

Tom Petty and The Heart-breakers
1755 Broadway, 8th Floor
New York, NY 10019

Rock group

U2
4 Windmill Lane
Dublin 4, Ireland

Rock group

Van Halen
3300 Warner Boulevard
Burbank, CA 91510

Rock group

Virgin Records America, Inc.
9247 Alden Drive
Beverly Hills, CA 90210
Jeff Ayeroff, co-managing director

Record label

Warner Brothers Records
75 Rockefeller Plaza, 20th Floor
New York, NY 10019
Mo Ostin, chairman

Recording company

Wilson Phillips
Chynna Phillips, Carnie Wilson, Wendy Wilson
1290 Avenue of the Americas
New York, NY 10104

Pop singing group

SPORTS FANS

Professional teams, amateur organizations, Halls of Fame, and circuses.

AAU/Carrier Youth Sports Programs
Amateur Athletic Union
3400 West 86th Street, P.O. Box 68207
Indianapolis, IN 46268
Jan Lyon, national program administrator
This is the nation's largest amateur multi-sport program, with training in twenty sports for kids 8–18.

Action Sports Association
15561 Product Lane, Suite D-8
Huntington Beach, CA 92649
Robert Morales, director
Provides safe, organized events for kids involved in action sports.

Akido Federation, Internationale
c/o Dr. Peter Goldsbury
Secretary General Adjoint FIA
Ushita Honmachi 3129
Four Chome Higashi-ku
Hiroshima 732, Japan
Doshu K. Uishiba, honorary president
International governing body for the sport of Akido.

All American Amateur Baseball Association
340 Walker Drive
Zanesville, OH 43701
Tom J. Checkush, executive director
Organized to foster, develop, and regulate amateur baseball.

Amateur Hockey Association of the United States
2997 Broadmoor Valley Road
Colorado Springs, CO 80906
Robert Johnson, executive director
National governing body for the sport of ice hockey.

Amateur Skating Union of the United States
1033 Shady Lane
Glen Ellyn, IL 60137
Shirley Yates, executive secretary

Group for people interested in speed skating, starting as young as 6 years old.

Amateur Softball Association
2801 N.E. 50th Street
Oklahoma City, OK 73111
Don E. Porter, executive director

The national governing body for the sport of softball in the US.

American Amateur Baseball Congress, Inc.
215 East Green Street, P.O. Box 467
Marshall, MI 49069
Joseph R. Cooper, president

Congress is made up of amateur baseball teams in six age divisions. Divisions are: Connie Mack, Mickey Mantle, Pee Wee Reese, Sandy Koufax, Stan Musial, and Willie Mays.

American Amateur Karate Federation
1930 Wilshire Boulevard
Suite 1208
Los Angeles, CA 90057
Hidetaka Nishiyama, president

The national governing body for Amateur karate in the US.

American Bicycle Association
P.O. Box 718
Chandler, AZ 85244
Clayton John, president

Promotes the sport of off-road bicycling (BMX).

American Bowling Congress
5301 South 76th Street
Greendale, WI 53129
Boyd M. Rexton, president

Governing body for amateur bowling.

American Canoe Association
8580 Cinderbed Road, Suite 1900
P.O. Box 1190
Newington, VA 22122–1190
David Mason, commodore

The national governing body for canoeing and kayaking in the US. Sponsors races.

American Double Dutch League
P.O. Box 776
Bronx, NY 10451
David Walker, founder

Organization for rope jumpers.

American Freestyle Association
15561 Product Lane, Suite D-8
Huntington Beach, CA 92649
Robert Morales, president

Promotes sport of freestyle bicycling and sanctions competitions.

American Hearing Impaired Hockey Association
1143 West Lake Street
Chicago, IL 60607
Stan Mikita, president

Promotes sport of amateur hockey among hearing-impaired young men, age 11 and up.

American Horse Shows Association
220 East 42nd Street, Suite 409
New York, NY 10017–5806
Chrystine Jones Tauber, executive vice-president
Sponsors junior equestrian competitions.

American Junior Golf Association
2415 Steeplechase Lane
Roswell, GA 30076
Stephen A. Hamblin, executive director
A golf association for young men and women under eighteen.

American Junior Rodeo Association
P.O. Box 481
Rankin, TX 79778
Leslie McFadden, secretary-manager
Sponsors rodeos for kids.

American Kitefliers Association
1559 Rockville Pike
Rockville, MD 10852
Jim Miller, president
Organization for anyone interested in kiteflying.

The American League of Professional Baseball Clubs
350 Park Avenue
New York, NY 10022
Dr. Robert W. Brown, MD, president

American Legion Baseball
American Legion National Headquarters
P.O. Box 1055
Indianapolis, IN 46206
Jim Quinlan, program coordinator
Baseball for teenagers sponsored by the American Legion and local businesses.

American Taekwondo Association
6210 Baseline Road
Little Rock, AR 72209
H. U. Lee, president
Sponsors competitions.

American Volkssport Association
Phoenix Square, Suite 203
10012 Pat Booker Road
Universal City, TX 78148
Tom Boyd, president
This is the governing body for regional, state, and local clubs that sponsor noncompetitive walking events.

American Youth Soccer Organization
5403 West 138th Street
Hawthorne, CA 90250
Timothy W. Thompson, national executive director
Sponsors competition for seven youth divisions.

Arizona Condors
4210 North Brown Avenue
Scottsdale, AZ 85251

Adrian Webster, general
manager
Soccer team

Athletes in Action
12084 Timberlake Drive
Cincinnati, OH 45242
Wendel Deyo, executive director
*The athletic program of Campus
Crusade for Christ. Runs sports
camps for kids.*

**The Athletic Congress of the
USA**
P.O. Box 120
Indianapolis, IN 46206
Ollan Cassell, executive director
*The national governing body for
track and field sports, long-
distance running, and race
walking.*

Atlanta Braves
P.O. Box 4064
Atlanta, GA 30302
Robert J. Cox, vice-president/
general manager
Professional baseball team

Atlanta Falcons
Suwanee Road at I–85
Suwanee, GA 30174
Rankin Smith, Jr., president
Professional football team

Atlanta Hawks
One CNN Center, Suite 405
South Tower
Atlanta, GA 30303
Stan Kasten, president/general
manager
Professional basketball team

Babe Ruth Baseball
1770 Brunswick Avenue, P.O.
Box 5000
Trenton, NJ 08638
Ronald Tellefson, president
Baseball for kids ages 8–18

Baltimore Orioles
Memorial Stadium
Baltimore, MD 21218
Roland D. Hemmond, vice-
president of Baseball Opera-
tions
Professional baseball team

Boston Bruins
Boston Garden
150 Causeway Street
Boston, MA 02114
Harry Sinden, president/general
manager
Professional hockey team

Boston Celtics
Boston Garden at North Station
150 Causeway Street
Boston, MA 02114
Jan Volk, executive vice-
president/general manager
Professional basketball team

Boston Red Sox
Fenway Park
24 Yawkey Way
Boston, MA 02215
James "Lou" Gorman, senior
vice-president/general man-
ager
Professional baseball team

Buffalo Bills
One Bills Drive
Orchard Park, NY 14127
Bill Polian, vice-president/
    general manager
Professional football team

Buffalo Sabres
Memorial Auditorium
140 Main Street
Buffalo, NY 14202
Gerry Meehan, general manager
Professional hockey team

Calgary Flames
Olympic Saddledome
P.O. Box 1540, Station M
Calgary, Alberta T2P 3B9
Canada
Cliff Fletcher, president/general
    manager
Professional hockey team

California Angels
P.O. Box 2000
Anaheim, CA 92803
Richard M. Brown, president
Professional baseball team

California Kickers
1755 East Martin Luther King, Jr.
    Boulevard
Los Angeles, CA 90058
Dan Foley, president
Soccer team

Charlotte Hornets
Two First Union Center, Suite
    2600
P.O. Box 30666
Charlotte, NC 28282

Carl Scheer, vice-president/
    general manager
Professional basketball team

Chicago Bears
Halas Hall
250 North Washington Road
Lake Forest, IL 60045
Michael B. McCaskey, president/
    CEO
Professional football team

Chicago Black Hawks
Chicago Stadium
1800 West Madison Street
Chicago, IL 60612
Robert Pulford, general manager
Professional hockey team

Chicago Bulls
980 North Michigan Avenue
Chicago, IL 60611
Jerry Krauss, vice-president
Professional basketball team

Chicago Cubs
Clark and Addison Streets
Chicago, IL 60613
James G. Frey, executive vice-
    president
Professional baseball team

Chicago White Sox
Comiskey Park
324 West 35th Street
Chicago, IL 60616
Larry Himes, senior vice-
    president/general manager
Professional baseball team

Cincinnati Bengals
200 Riverfront Stadium
Cincinnati, OH 45202
Paul E. Brown, general manager
Professional football team

Cincinnati Reds
100 Riverfront Stadium
Cincinnati, OH 45202
Bob Quin, vice-president/general
   manager
Professional baseball team

Cinderella Softball Leagues
P.O. Box 1411
Corning, NY 14830
Tony Maio, president
*Conducts softball leagues for
girls under 18.*

Cirque du Soleil
1217 Notre-Dame Street E
Montreal, QUE H2L 2R3
Canada
Circus

Cleveland Browns
Cleveland Stadium
Cleveland, OH 44114
Ernie Accorsi, executive vice-
   president
Professional football team

Cleveland Cavaliers
2923 Statesboro Road
Richfield, OH 44286
Wayne Embry, vice-president/
   general manager
Professional basketball team

Cleveland Indians
Cleveland Stadium
Cleveland, OH 44114
Dennis Lehman, senior vice-
   president
Professional baseball team

Colorado Foxes
6735 Stroh Road
Parker, CO 80134
Greg Todd, general manager
Soccer team

Dallas Cowboys
One Cowboys Parkway
Irving, TX 75063
Jerry Jones, president
Professional football team

Dallas Mavericks
Reunion Arena
777 Sports Street
Dallas, TX 75207
Norm Sonju, general manager/
   COO
Professional basketball team

Denver Broncos
5700 Logan Street
Denver, CO 80216
John Beake, general manager
Professional football team

Denver Nuggets
P.O. Box 4658
Denver, CO 80204
Jon Spoelstra, president/general
   manager
Professional basketball team

Detroit Lions
Pontiac Silverdome
1200 Featherstone Road
P.O. Box 4200
Pontiac, MI 48057
Russell Thomas, executive vice-president/general manager
Professional football team

Detroit Pistons
One Championship Drive
Auburn Hills, MI 48057
Jack McCloskey, general manager
Professional basketball team

Detroit Red Wings
Joe Louis Arena
600 Civic Center Drive
Detroit, MI 48226
Jim Devellano, president/general manager
Professional hockey team

Detroit Tigers
Tiger Stadium
Michigan and Trumbull Avenues
Detroit, MI 48216
Jim Campbell, president
Professional baseball team

Direction Sports
117 West 9th Street, Suite 520
Los Angeles, CA 90015
Tulley N. Brown, executive director
Program which gives kids something to do so they can feel positive about themselves and those around them. De-signed for inner-city housing project kids.

Edmonton Oilers
Northlands Coliseum
7424–118 Avenue
Edmonton, Alberta T5B 4M9
Canada
Glen Sather, president/general manager
Professional hockey team

George Khoury Association of Baseball Leagues
5400 Meramec Bottom Road
St. Louis, MO 63128
George G. Khoury, executive director
Leagues for boys and girls age 7 and older organized by local churches.

Global Wrestling Federation
1692 Sprinter Street, NW
Atlanta, GA 30318
Joe Pedicino, president
Professional wrestling association

Golden Gloves Association of America, Inc.
1503 Linda Lane
Hutchinson, KS 67502
Jim Beasley, secretary/treasurer
Boxing competition for teenagers

Golden State Warriors
The Oakland Coliseum Arena
Nimitz Freeway and Hegenberger Road

Oakland, CA 94621
Daniel F. Finnane, president
Professional basketball team

Green Bay Packers
1265 Lombardi Avenue
Green Bay, WI 54303
Robert E. Harlan, president/CEO
Professional football team

Harlem Globetrotters
6121 Sunset Boulevard
Los Angeles, CA 90038
Comedy basketball team

Hartford Whalers
One Civic Center Plaza
Hartford, CT 06103
Eddie Johnston, vice-president/
    general manager
Professional hockey team

Houston Astros
P.O. Box 288
Houston, TX 77001
Bill Wood, general manager
Professional baseball team

Houston Oilers
6910 Fannin Street
Houston, TX 77030
Mike Holovak, general manager
Professional football team

Houston Rockets
The Summit
Houston, TX 77046
Ray Patterson, president
Professional basketball team

Ice Skating Institute of America
1000 Skokie Boulevard
Wilmette, IL 60091
Justine Townsend Smith, executive director
Dedicated to providing quality ice-skating programs for the community and the recreational skater.

Indiana Pacers
Market Square Arena
300 East Market Street
Indianapolis, IN 46204
Donnie Walsh, president
Professional basketball team

Indianapolis Colts
7001 West 56th Street
P.O. Box 53500
Indianapolis, IN 46253
James Irsay, vice-president/
    general manager
Professional football team

International Cheerleading Foundation
10660 Barkley
Shawnee Mission, KS 66212
Randolph L. Neil, president
Sponsors cheerleading competitions.

International Gymnastic Hall of Fame
227 Brooks Street
Oceanside, CA 92054
Glenn M. Sundby, director

International Hockey Hall of Fame and Museum
York and Alfred Streets
Box 82
Kingston, ON K7L 4V6 Canada
Doug Nichols, executive director

International Soap Box Derby
789 Derby Downs Drive
Akron, OH 44306
Jeff Iula, general manager

The organization for the soap box derby, founded in 1933.

International Sport Karate Association
Box 44095
Denver, CO 80201
Karyn Turner, commissioner

Kickboxing association

International Surfing Hall of Fame
5580 La Jolla Boulevard, Suite 373
La Jolla, CA 92037
Lois Ronaldson, president

International Swimming Hall of Fame
One Hall of Fame Drive
Fort Lauderdale, FL 33316
Dr. Sam Frees, executive director

IronKids Club
P.O. Box 660217
Dallas, TX 75266–0217

A program modeled on the "Iron Man" competitions for kids ages 7–14. Holds mini-triathlons in some US cities.

Junior Bowhunter Program
National Field Archery Association
31407 Outer Interstate 10
Redlands, CA 92373
Pam Shilling, contact

Archery program for young hunters. Write to them, and they will provide you with the name of a contact in your state who will help you find a local club.

Junior Club
National Rifle Association of America
1600 Rhode Island Avenue, NW
Washington, DC 20036
Grace Albert, Sports Department

The Junior club provides qualification courses in riflery and a home firearms responsibility program.

Junior Olympic Archery Development
National Archery Association
1750 East Boulder Street
Colorado Springs, CO 80909
Christine McCartney, executive director

Archery program for competitive target shooting.

Kansas City Chiefs
One Arrowhead Drive
Kansas City, MO 64129
Carl Peterson, president/general manager

Professional football team

Kansas City Royals
P.O. Box 419969
Kansas City, MO 64141
John Schuerholz, executive vice-
president/general manager
Professional baseball team

**Knights Boxing Team-
International**
560 Campbell Hill
Marietta, GA 30061
Don Wade, executive director
*Seeks to promote the sport of
boxing as an alternative to
drugs, alcohol, and crime, for
boys 12 and older.*

**Lacrosse Hall of Fame and
Museum
Lacrosse Foundation, Inc.**
Newton H. White Athletic Center
Baltimore, MD 21218
James L. Potter, president

League of American Wheelmen
6707 Whitestone Road, Suite
209
Baltimore, MD 21207
John Cornelison, executive director
*Promotes safe bicycling as a
form of recreation and as transportation.*

Little League Baseball, Inc.
P.O. Box 3485
Williamsport, PA 17701
Dr. Creighton J. Hale, president
*Organized baseball league in all
US states and territories and 29
foreign countries for boys and*

*girls ages 6–18. Sponsors Inter-
national World Series in August.*

Los Angeles Clippers
LA Memorial Sports Arena
3939 South Figueroa Avenue
Los Angeles, CA 90037
Elgin Baylor, executive vice-
president/general manager
Professional basketball team

Los Angeles Dodgers
1000 Elysian Park Avenue
Los Angeles, CA 90012
Peter O'Malley, president
Professional baseball team

Los Angeles Heat
220 South Pacific Coast High-
way, #104
Redondo Beach, CA 90277
Dan Olsen, chairman
Soccer team

Los Angeles Kings
The Forum
P.O. Box 17013
Inglewood, CA 90308
Rogie Vachon, general manager
Professional hockey team

Los Angeles Lakers
P.O. Box 10
Inglewood, CA 90306
Jerry West, general manager
Professional basketball team

Los Angeles Raiders
332 Center Street
El Segundo, CA 90245
Al Davis, managing general part-
ner
Professional football team

Los Angeles Rams
2327 West Lincoln Avenue
Anaheim, CA 92801
Georgia Frontiere, president
Professional football team

Miami Dolphins
2269 NW 199th Street
Miami, FL 33056
J. Michael Robbie, executive vice-
president/general manager
Professional football team

Miami Heat
Miami Arena
Miami, FL 33136–4102
Lewis Schaffel, managing part-
ner
Professional basketball team

Milwaukee Brewers
Milwaukee County Stadium
Milwaukee, WI 53214
Harry Dalton, vice-president/
general manager
Professional baseball team

Milwaukee Bucks
1001 North 4th Street
Milwaukee, WI 53203
John Steinmiller, vice-president
Professional basketball team

Mini-Hockey
Field Hockey Association of
America
1750 East Boulder Street
Colorado Springs, CO 80909
Ed Cliatt, executive director
*Field hockey program for young
men*

Minnesota North Stars
Met Center
7901 Cedar Avenue South
Bloomington, MN 55425
Jack Fereirra, vice-president/
general manager
Professional hockey team

Minnesota Timberwolves
500 City Place
730 Hennepin Avenue, Suite 500
Minneapolis, MN 55403
Bob Stein, president
Professional basketball team

Minnesota Twins
Hubert H. Humphrey Metro-
dome
501 Chicago Avenue, South
Minneapolis, MN 55415
Andy McPhail, executive vice-
president/general manager
Professional baseball team

Minnesota Vikings
9520 Viking Drive
Eden Prairie, MN 55344
Mike Lynn, executive vice-
president/general manager
Professional football team

Montreal Canadiens
2313 Ste. Catherine West
Montreal, QUE H3H 1N2
Canada
Fred Steer, vice-president
Professional hockey team

Montreal Expos
P.O. Box 500, Station M
Montreal, QUE H1V 3P2
Canada
Bill Stoneman, vice-president
Professional baseball team

Naismith Memorial Basketball Hall of Fame
P.O. Box 179
1150 West Columbus Avenue
Springfield, MA 01101–0179
Bob Cousy, president

National Amateur Baseball Federation
12406 Keynote Lane
Bowie, MD 20715
Charles M. Blackburn, executive director
Has four age groups of organized baseball. Specializes in non-commercial baseball.

National Association of Police Athletic Leagues
200 Castlewood Drive
North Palm Beach, FL 33408
Joseph F. Johnson, executive director
This group sponsors national tournaments in boxing, basketball, baseball, softball, soccer, field hockey, and Tae Kwon Do.

National Association of Scuba Diving Schools
641 West Willow Street
Long Beach, CA 90806
John Geffney, executive director

National Baseball Hall of Fame and Museum, Inc.
Box 590
Cooperstown, NY 13326
Edward W. Stack, president

National Basketball Association
645 Fifth Avenue
New York, NY 10022
David J. Stern, commissioner

National Baton Twirling Association, International
P.O. Box 266
Janesville, WI 53545
Don Sartell, president
Association of twirlers

National Bicycle League
211 Bradenton Avenue, Suite 100
P.O. Box 729
Dublin, OH 43017
Bob Tedesco, chief executive officer
Motorcross racing for kids as young as 3 years old.

National Bowling Hall of Fame and Museum
111 Stadium Plaza
St. Louis, MO 63102
R. R. Woodruff, president

The National Football Foundation and Hall of Fame Inc.
Hall of Fame
King's Island, OH 45045
Dick Craig, general manager

National Football League
410 Park Avenue
New York, NY 10022
Paul Tagliabue, commissioner

National Football League Player's Association
AFL-CIO
2021 L Street, NW
Washington, DC 20036
Gene Upshaw, executive director

Labor union for professional football players

National High School Rodeo Association
c/o Bill Atchison
128 North Second Street
Douglas, WY 82633
Bill Atchison, acting secretary

Aims to develop sportsmanship, horsemanship, and character in youth. Participants must also meet academic standards set by the association.

National Hockey League
650 Fifth Avenue, 33rd Floor
New York, NY 10019
William B. Wirtz, chairman of the board

National Hot Rod Association
2035 Financial Way
Glendora, CA 91740

Dallas Gardner, president

Promotes interest in construction and racing of modified and special-built automobiles.

The National League of Professional Baseball Clubs
350 Park Avenue
New York, NY 10022
William White, president

National Little Britches Rodeo Association
1045 West Rio Grande
Colorado Springs, CO 80906
Jim Chamley, general manager

Sponsors rodeos for kids ages 8–18

National Scholastic Surfing Association
P.O. Box 495
Huntington Beach, CA 82648
Janice Aragon, executive director

Surfing association for students

National Teenage Team Racquetball
5089 North Granite Reef Road
Scottsdale, AZ 85253
Mort Leve, executive director

Racquetball league for teenagers

New England Patriots
Sullivan Stadium
Route 1
Foxboro, MA 02035
Patrick J. Sullivan, general manager

Professional football team

New Jersey Devils
Byrne Meadowlands Arena
East Rutherford, NJ 07073
Lou Lamoriello, president/
general manager
Professional hockey team

New Jersey Nets
Brendan Byrne Meadowlands
Arena
East Rutherford, NJ 07073
Bernie Mann, president
Professional basketball team

New Mexico Chiles
1501 12th Street, NW, Suite 108
Albuquerque, NM 87104
David Carr, general manager
Soccer team

New Orleans Saints
6928 Saints Avenue
Metairie, LA 70003
Jim Finks, president/general
manager
Professional football team

New York Giants
Giants Stadium
East Rutherford, NJ 07073
George Young, vice-president/
general manager
Professional football team

New York Islanders
Nassau Veterans Memorial
Coliseum
Hempstead Turnpike
Uniondale, NY 11553
William A. Torrey, chairman of
the board/general manager

Professional hockey team

New York Jets
598 Madison Avenue
New York, NY 10022
Steve Gutman, president/COO
Professional football team

New York Knickerbockers
Four Penn Plaza
New York, NY 10001
Al Bianchi, vice-president/
general manager
Professional basketball team

New York Mets
126th and Roosevelt Avenue
Flushing, NY 11368
J. Frank Cashen, executive vice-
president/general manager
Professional baseball team

New York Rangers
Madison Square Garden
Four Penn Plaza
New York, NY 10001
Neil Smith, vice-president/
general manager
Professional hockey team

New York Yankees
Yankee Stadium
Bronx, NY 10451
Harding "Pete" Peterson, general
manager
Professional baseball team

Oakland Athletics
Oakland-Alameda County
  Stadium
Oakland, CA 94621
Roy Esenhardt, executive vice-
  president
Professional baseball team

Orlando Magic
Orlando Arena
One Magic Place
Orlando, FL 32801
Pat Williams, president/general
  manager
Professional basketball team

Philadelphia Eagles
Veterans Stadium
Broad Street and Pattison
Philadelphia, PA 19148
Harry Gamble, president/COO
Professional football team

Philadelphia Flyers
The Spectrum—Pattison Place
Philadelphia, PA 19148
Bobby Clark, vice-president/
  general manager
Professional hockey team

Philadelphia Phillies
P.O. Box 7575
Philadelphia, PA 19101
David Montgomery, executive
  vice-president
Professional baseball team

Philadelphia 76ers
Veterans Stadium
P.O. Box 25040
Philadelphia, PA 19147

John Nash, general manager
Professional basketball team

Phoenix Cardinals
P.O. Box 888
Phoenix, AZ 85001
Joe Rhein, executive vice-
  president
Professional football team

Phoenix Suns
2910 North Central Avenue
P.O. Box 1369
Phoenix, AZ 85001
Jerry Colangelo, president/CEO
Professional basketball team

Pittsburgh Penguins
Gate Number 9, Civic Arena
Pittsburgh, PA 15219
Craig Patrick, general manager
Professional hockey team

Pittsburgh Pirates
600 Stadium Circle
Pittsburgh, PA 15212
Larry Doughty, senior vice-
  president/general manager
Professional baseball team

Pittsburgh Steelers
Three Rivers Stadium
300 Stadium Circle
Pittsburgh, PA 15212
Daniel M. Rooney, president
Professional football team

Pony of the Americas Club, Inc.
5240 Elmwood Avenue
Indianapolis, IN 46203
Clyde Goff, executive secretary

Association of forty member clubs, who conduct 300 horse shows annually.

Pony Baseball
P.O. Box 225
Washington, PA 15301
Roy Gillespie, president
Six baseball divisions for boys ages 7–18. Also sponsors softball leagues for girls.

Pop Warner Football
1315 Walnut Street, Suite 1632
Philadelphia, PA 19107
David Glenn Warner Tomlin, president
Various leagues for age groups ranging from 7–16.

Portland Timbers
10725 SW Barbur Boulevard, Suite 390
Portland, OR 97219
Art Dixon, president
Soccer team

Portland Trail Blazers
700 Northeast Multnomah Street
Lloyd Building, Suite 600
Portland, OR 97232
Harry Glickman, president
Professional basketball team

President's Council on Physical Fitness and Sports
450 5th Street, NW, Suite 7103
Washington, DC 20001
Steve Guback, director of information

This council was formed by President Eisenhower to encourage physical fitness and participation in sports.

Pro Football Hall of Fame
2121 George Halas Drive, NW
Canton, OH 44708
Peter R. Elliott, president/ executive director

Professional Bowler's Association of America
1720 Merriman Road
P.O. Box 5118
Akron, OH 44313
John Petraglia, president

Professional Golfers' Association Hall of Fame
P.O. Box 109601
100 Avenue of the Champions
Palm Beach Gardens, FL 33418
Gary Wiren, director

Professional Surfing Association of America
530 Sixth Street
Hermosa Beach, CA 90254
L. Malek, marketing director

Quebec Nordiques
Colisee de Quebec
2205 Avenue du Colisee
Quebec, QUE G1L 4W7
Canada
Martin Madden, general manager
Professional hockey team

Real Santa Barbara
105 East De La Guerra, Suite 4
Santa Barbara, CA 93101
C. Paul Davis, general manager
Soccer team

Ringling Brothers Circus
P.O. Box 2366
L'Enfant Plaza Street
Washington, DC 20026
Kenneth Feld, president

Sacramento Kings
One Sports Parkway
Sacramento, CA 95834
Joe Axelson, executive vice-
president
Professional basketball team

Sacramento Senators
4010 Foothill Boulevard, Suite
104
Roseville, CA 95678
Greg McKeown, chairman
Soccer team

Salt Lake City
c/o Salt Lake City Trappers
1301 SW Temple
Salt Lake City, UT 84115
Mark Hugo, general manager
Soccer team

San Antonio Spurs
600 East Market Street,
Suite 102
San Antonio, TX 78205
Russ Bookbinder, executive vice-
president
Professional basketball team

San Diego Chargers
Jack Murphy Stadium
P.O. Box 20666
San Diego, CA 92120
Steve Ortmayer, director of foot-
ball operations
Professional football team

San Diego Nomads
1298 Prospect Street
La Jolla, CA 92037
James Jessel, general manager
Soccer team

San Diego Padres
P.O. Box 2000
San Diego, CA 92120
Dick Freeman, president
Professional baseball team

San Francisco Bay Blackhawks
3820 Blackhawk Road
Danville, CA 94506
Terry Fisher, general manager
Soccer team

San Francisco 49ers
4949 Centennial Boulevard
Santa Clara, CA 95054–1229
Edward J. DeBartolo, Jr., owner/
president
Professional football team

San Francisco Giants
Candlestick Park
San Francisco, CA 94124
Al Rosen, president/general
manager
Professional baseball team

Scholastic Rowing Association of America
c/o Davis Washburn, secretary
St. Andrew's School
Middletown, DE 19709
Glendon E. Robertson, president
Rowing association for students

Seattle Mariners
P.O. Box 4100
Seattle, WA 98104
Woody Woodward, vice-
    president/general manager
Professional baseball team

Seattle Seahawks
11220 NE 53rd Street
Kirkland, WA 98033
Tom Flores, general manager
Professional football team

Seattle Storm
2815 Second Avenue, Suite 590
Seattle, WA 98121
David Gillett, general manager
Soccer team

Seattle SuperSonics
C-Box 900911
Seattle, WA 98109
Bob Whitsitt, president
Professional basketball team

Soccer Association for Youth
5945 Ridge Avenue
Cincinnati, OH 45213
James H. Gruenwald, executive
    director
Organizes special youth soccer competitions. Does not make judgments on a player's ability; all kids get to play.

Special Olympics International
1350 New York Avenue, NW,
    Suite 500
Washington, DC 20005
Eunice Kennedy Shriver, chair-
person
A year-round, worldwide program of training and competition in 22 sports for mentally retarded citizens ages 8 and over. Sponsors International Summer and Winter Special Olympics.

St. Louis Blues
The Arena
5700 Oakland Avenue
St. Louis, MO 63110
Jack Quinn, president
Professional hockey team

St. Louis Cardinals
250 Stadium Plaza
St. Louis, MO 63102
Dal Maxvill, vice-president/
    general manager
Professional baseball team

Tampa Bay Buccaneers
One Buccaneer Place
Tampa, FL 33607
Hugh F. Culverhouse, owner
Professional football team

Texas Rangers
1250 Copeland Road, Suite
    1100
Arlington, TX 76011

Thomas A. Grieve, vice-president/general manager

Professional baseball team

Toronto Blue Jays
300 The Esplanade West, Suite 3200
Toronto, ON M5V 3B3
Canada
Paul Beeston, president/COO

Professional baseball team

Toronto Maple Leafs
Maple Leaf Gardens
60 Carlton Street
Toronto, ON M5B 1L1
Canada
Harold E. Ballard, president

Professional hockey team

United States Amateur Confederation of Roller Skating
P.O. Box 6579
1500 South 70th Street
Lincoln, NE 68506
Len Taylor, public information director

Governing body for the sport of roller skating in the US.

United States Baseball Federation
2160 Greenwood Avenue
Trenton, NJ 08609
Scott Bollwage, development director

In the years when the Olympics are not held, this group organizes the Junior National Team, which plays internationally.

United States Bicycling Hall of Fame and Museum
P.O. Box 1111
Sommerville, NJ 08876

United States Diving, Inc.
201 South Capitol Avenue, Suite 430
Indianapolis, IN 46225
Todd B. Smith, executive director

Sponsors competitive youth diving programs for ages 10–18.

United States Fencing Association
1750 East Boulder Street
Colorado Springs, CO 80909
Carla-Mae Richards, executive director

This association has three levels of youth participation: Youth, Cadet, and Junior. It is also responsible for selecting the US team for international competitions.

United States Figure Skating Association
20 First Street
Colorado Springs, CO 80906
Ian Anderson, executive director

National governing body for the sport of amateur figure skating.

United States Gymnastics Federation
Pan American Plaza
201 South Capitol, Suite 300
Indianapolis, IN 46225
Mike Jacki, executive director

Governing body for gymnastics in the US; they select the US national team for international competition.

United States International Speedskating Association

240 Oneida Street
Syracuse, NY 13204
John Byrne, executive officer

Supports speedskating in the US and organizes teams for international competition.

United States Judo, Inc.

P.O. Box 10013
El Paso, TX 79991
Frank Fullerton, president

Governing body for amateur judo in the US.

United States Junior National Cycling Program

United States Cycling Federation
1750 East Boulder Street
Colorado Springs, CO 80909
Bob Bill, junior national coach

Sponsors cycling programs and competitions, and selects national junior teams to compete internationally.

United States Lifesaving Association

425 East McFetridge Drive
Chicago, IL 60605
Ray Colonna, executive director

Association of lifeguards.

United States Luge Association

P.O. Box 651
Lake Placid, NY 12946
Lin Hancock, junior development director

Junior program for youth ages 12–18.

United States Paddle Tennis Association

Box 30
Culver City, CA 90232
Greg Lawrence, president

Sponsors competitions.

United States Pony Clubs, Inc.

893 South Matlack Street, Suite 210
West Chester, PA 19382–4913
Susan Giddings, national administrator

Sponsors competition for members up to age 21 and offers exchange programs with members of clubs overseas.

United States Rowing Association

201 South Capitol Avenue, Suite 400
Indianapolis, IN 46225
Paula Oyer, executive director

Rowing clubs from colleges, universities, prep schools, and other high schools. Creates and enforces rules.

United States Ski Association
P.O. Box 100
Park City, UT 84060
Howard Peterson, executive
 officer
*The governing body for amateur
skiing in the US.*

United States Soccer Federation
United States Youth Soccer Asso-
 ciation
1835 Union Avenue, Suite 190
Memphis, TN 38104
Mavis Derflinger, chairman
*The youth division of the US
Soccer Federation.*

**United States Surfing Federa-
tion**
National Scholastic Surfing Asso-
 ciation
P.O. Box 495
Huntington Beach, CA 92648
Janice Aragon, executive director
*Teen subsidiary of the US Surf-
ing Federation.*

United States Swimming, Inc.
1750 East Boulder Street
Colorado Springs, CO 80909
Ray B. Essick, executive director
*National governing body for
swimming in the US, conducts
program for kids ages 5 and up.*

**United States Synchronized
Swimming, Inc.**
201 South Capitol Avenue, Suite
 510
Indianapolis, IN 46225

Betty Watanabe, executive
 director
*Conducts age-graded programs
for swimmers ages 10 and up.
Has affiliated clubs in local
areas.*

**United States Table Tennis
Association**
1750 East Boulder Street
Colorado Springs, CO 80909
Larry Hodges, youth program
 coordinator
Scott Preiss, coordinator, Boys
 Clubs Programs
*Ping-Pong program used in
schools and boys clubs.*

**United States Tae Kwon Do
Union**
1750 East Boulder Street
Colorado Springs, CO 80909
Kay Flora, business director
*Sponsors junior competitive
events for kids ages 6–17.*

**United States Team Handball
Federation**
1750 East Boulder Street
Colorado Springs, CO 80909
Mike Cavanaugh, executive
 director
*Sponsors a competitive pro-
gram for junior and senior high
school students.*

**United States Tennis
Association**
National Junior Tennis League
707 Alexander Road
Princeton, NJ 08540

Beth Brainard, coordinator of program development

Tennis association for kids

United States Twirling Association

P.O. Box 24488
Seattle, WA 98124
Kathy Forsythe, administrative coordinator

Promotes baton twirling as both a recreational and competitive sport.

United States Weightlifting Federation

1750 East Boulder Street
Colorado Springs, CO 80909
George Greenway, executive director

The national governing body for weightlifting in the US

United States Youth Soccer Association

7112 Whetstone Road
Alexandria, VA 22306
Mavis Derflinger, chairman

Youth organization affiliated with the US Soccer Federation.

USA Amateur Boxing Federation

1750 East Boulder Street
Colorado Springs, CO 80909
Bruce Mathis, associate executive director

Sponsors boxing tournaments for 8–15-year-olds.

USA Junior Field Hockey

USA Field Hockey Association
1750 East Boulder Street
Colorado Springs, CO 80909–5773
Beth Vasta, U.S.A. Junior Hockey director

Purpose of this organization is to introduce and promote field hockey among 5–13-year-olds.

USA Karate Federation Junior Olympics

The USA Karate Federation
1300 Kenmore Boulevard
Akron, OH 44314
Jeff Ellis, director, Junior Programs

Organizes graded competitive program for youth in elementary through high school; culminates in Junior Olympics.

USA Wrestling

255 South Academy Boulevard
Colorado Springs, CO 80901
David C. Miller, executive director

USA Wrestling Kids Division for youth ages 14 and under, other divisions for older kids.

USA Youth Volleyball Program
USA Junior Olympic Volleyball

United States Volleyball Association
1750 East Boulder Street
Colorado Springs, CO 80909
Clifford T. McPeak, executive director

The national governing body for the sport of volleyball.

Utah Jazz
5 Triad Center
Salt Lake City, UT 84180
Frank Layden, president
Professional basketball team

Vancouver Canucks
Pacific Coliseum
100 North Renfrew Street
Vancouver, BC V5K 3N7
Canada
Pat Quinn, president/general
    manager
Professional hockey team

Washington Bullets
One Harry S. Truman Drive
Landover, MD 20785
Bob Ferry, vice-president/
    general manager
Professional basketball team

Washington Capitals
Capital Centre
Landover, MD 20785
David Poile, vice-president/
    general manager
Professional hockey team

Washington Redskins
Redskin Park
P.O. Box 17247
Dulles International Airport
Washington, DC 20041
John Kent Cooke, executive vice-
    president
Professional football team

Western Soccer League
2815 Second Avenue, Suite 300
Seattle, WA 98121
William C. Sage, chairman
Association of soccer teams

Winnipeg Jets
Winnipeg Arena
15–1430 Maroons Road
Winnipeg, MAN R3G OL5
Canada
Barry Shenkarow, president
Professional hockey team

Women's International Bowling Congress, Inc.
5301 South 76th Street
Greendale, WI 53129
Gladys Banker, president
Bowling league which sponsors programs for girls.

Women's Professional Rodeo Association
Route 5, Box 698
Blanchard, OK 73010
Lydia Moore, secretary-treasurer
Organization of women's barrel racers; not strictly for youth, but over 10 percent of the members are under 18.

World Championship Wrestling, Inc.
(a subsidiary of Turner Broadcasting)
P.O. Box 105366
Atlanta, GA 30348–5366
Ted Turner, CEO

Professional wrestling organization

The World Figure Skating Hall of Fame and Museum
20 First Street
Colorado Springs, CO 80906–3697
Ian Anderson, executive director

World Wrestling Federation
c/o Titan Sports
1055 Summer Street
P.O. Box 3857
Stamford, CT 06905

Vincent K. McMahon, president/CEO

Professional wrestling association

Young American Bowling Alliance
5301 South 76th Street
Greendale, WI 53129
E. J. Clarkson, executive director

Sponsors tournaments for kids.

ON THE TUBE AND ON THE SCREEN

Your favorite television programs are listed by name, as well as the people who make them. Television networks and major movie companies are in this category, too.

A & E
Arts and Entertainment Network
555 Fifth Avenue
New York, NY 10017
Nick Davatzes, CEO

Cable network

A Different World
The Carsey-Werner Company
4024 Radford Avenue, #3
Studio City, CA 91604
Marcy Carsey, Tom Werner, executive producers

NBC sitcom

**ABC Television Network
a division of Capitol Cities/ABC
Incorporated**
77 West 66th Street
New York, NY 10023
Thomas S. Murphy, chairman

American Gladiators
Four Point Entertainment
3575 Cahuenga Boulevard,
　#600

Los Angeles, CA 90068
Ron Ziskin, executive producer

Syndicated sports competition

America's Funniest Home Videos
Vin Di Bona Productions
4151 Prospect Avenue
Hollywood, CA 90027
Vin Di Bona, executive producer

ABC series hosted by Bob Saget

America's Funniest People
Vin Di Bona Productions
4151 Prospect Avenue
Hollywood, CA 90027
Vin Di Bona, executive producer

ABC series

Arbitron Company
3333 Wilshire Boulevard, Suite
　712
Los Angeles, CA 90012
Rick Aurichio, president

TV ratings company

Armed Forces Radio & Television Broadcast Center
10888 La Tuna Canyon Road
Sun Valley, CA 91352
Colonel Richard Fuller, commander

Radio and television network for the armed forces.

Beatlejuice
Nelvana Entertainment
9000 Sunset Boulevard, Suite 911
Los Angeles, CA 90069
Lenora Hume, supervising producer

ABC animated series

Beverly Hills 90210
Spelling Entertainment Inc.
5700 Wilshire Boulevard, Suite 575
Los Angeles, CA 90036
Charles Rosin, executive producer

Fox Network series

Blossom
Witt/Thomas Productions
846 North Cahuenga Boulevard
Hollywood, CA 90038
Paul Junger Witt, Tony Thomas, Don Reo, executive producers

NBC series

Bravo Cable Network
150 Crossways Park West
Woodbury, NY 11797
Joshua Sapan, president

Cable network that airs classical concerts, foreign films, and documentaries.

Brooklyn Bridge
Paramount Network Television Productions
5555 Melrose Avenue
Hollywood, CA 90038
Gary David Goldberg, executive producer

CBS series

The Bugs Bunny and Tweety Show
Warner Brothers Animation Inc.
15303 Ventura Boulevard, Suite 1100
Sherman Oaks, CA 91403
Kathleen Helppie-Shippley, executive producer

ABC animated series

Cable News Network (CNN)
One CNN Center, P.O. Box 105366
Atlanta, GA 30348–5366
W. Thomas Johnson, president

Cable Satellite Public Affairs Network (C-SPAN)
400 North Capitol Street, NW, Suite 650
Washington, DC 20001
Brian Lamb, chairman/CEO

Cable channel that broadcasts Senate and House of Representatives sessions.

The Cannell Studios
7083 Hollywood Boulevard
Hollywood, CA 90028
Stephen J. Cannell, chairman of the board & CEO

Television program production company

Captain N: The Game Master
DIC Enterprises Inc.
3601 West Olive Avenue
Burbank, CA 91505
Andy Heyward, executive producer

NBC animated series

Captain Planet and the Planeteers
DIC Enterprises, Inc.
3601 West Olive Avenue
Burbank, CA 91505
Andy Heyward, executive producer

TBS animated series

Carolco Pictures Inc.
8800 Sunset Boulevard
Los Angeles, CA 90069
Mario F. Kassar, chairman of the board

Movie production company

Castle Rock Entertainment
335 North Maple Drive, Suite 135
Beverly Hills, CA 90210
Rob Reiner, principal and co-founder

Movie production company

CBS Inc.
524 West 57th Street
New York, NY 10019
Laurence Tisch, chairman/CEO

Television network

Children's Television Workshop
One Lincoln Plaza
New York, NY 10023
David Britt, president

Produces programs for children, including "Sesame Street," "Square One TV," and "3-2-1 Contact."

Chip & Pepper's Cartoon Madness
DIC Enterprises, Inc.
3601 West Olive Avenue
Burbank, CA 91505
Andy Heyward, executive producer

NBC animated series

Christian Broadcasting Network, Incorporated (CBN)
1000 Centerville Turnpike
Virginia Beach, VA 23463
Pat Robertson, president

Religious cable network

Cinemax
1100 Avenue of the Americas
New York, NY 10036
Michael Fuchs, chairman/CEO

Cable premium movie channel

Columbia Pictures
Columbia Studios

10202 West Washington Boulevard
Culver City, CA 90232
Frank Price, chairman

Movie production company

The Comedy Channel (an HBO Company)

120 East 23rd Street
New York, NY 10010
Michael Fuchs, chairman/CEO

Cable channel

The Congressional Award

6520 Georgetown Pike
McLean, VA 22101
Kendall S. Hartman, national director

Through the combined efforts of Congress and the private sector, Congressional Awards may be earned by young people ages 14–23 who fulfill national requirements.

The Cosby Show

The Carsey-Werner Company
4024 Radford Avenue, #3
Studio City, CA 91604
Marcy Carsey, Tom Werner, Janet Leahy, executive producers

NBC sitcom

Crown International Pictures, Inc.

8701 Wilshire Boulevard
Beverly Hills, CA 90211
Mark Tenser, president/CEO

Movie production company

Darkwing Duck

Buena Vista Television
5200 Lankershim Boulevard
North Hollywood, CA 91601
Tad Stones, supervising producer

Animated television series

The Discovery Channel

7700 Wisconsin Avenue
Bethesda, MD 20814
Ruth Ott, president

Cable channel that broadcasts travel films and documentaries.

The Disney Channel

3800 West Alameda Avenue
Burbank, CA 91505
John F. Cooke, president

Mouse-owned cable channel

Doogie Howser, M.D.

Steven Bochco Productions
P.O. Box 900
Beverly Hills, CA 90213
Vic Rauseo, Linda Morris, executive producers

ABC series

E! Entertainment Television, Inc.

5670 Wilshire Boulevard, 2nd Floor
Los Angeles, CA 90036
Lee Masters, president/CEO

Cable network that airs interviews with celebrities, film reviews, and entertainment-oriented documentaries.

ESPN, Incorporated
ESPN Plaza
Bristol, CT 06010
Steven Bornstein, president
Cable sports channel

The Family Channel
1000 Centerville Turnpike
Virginia Beach, VA 23463
Tim Robertson, president/CEO
Cable channel with family programming and classic repeats.

FamilyNet
P.O. Box 196
Forest, VA 24551–0196
David Lewis, marketing manager
Family programming network

Fish Police
Hanna-Barbera Productions, Inc.
3400 Cahuenga Boulevard
Hollywood, CA 90068
David Kirschner, executive producer
CBS animated series

**Fox Broadcasting Company
a division of Fox Incorporated**
10201 West Pico Boulevard
Los Angeles, CA 90035
Jamie Kellner, president
Small television network

The Fresh Prince of Bel Air
NBC Productions
330 Bob Hope Drive
Burbank, CA 91523
Winifred Hervey, Quincy Jones, executive producers
NBC sitcom

Full House
Lorimar Television
300 South Lorimar Plaza
Burbank, CA 91505
Jeff Franklin, Thomas L. Miller, Robert L. Boyett, executive producers
ABC series

Garfield and Friends
Film Roman
12020 Chandler Boulevard, #200
North Hollywood, CA 91607
Phil Roman, executive producer
CBS animated series

Ghostwriter
Children's Television Workshop
One Lincoln Plaza
New York, NY 10023
Liz Nealon, executive producer
PBS series

Growing Pains
Warner Brothers Television
4000 Warner Boulevard
Burbank, CA 91522
Dan Wilcox, executive producer
ABC series

Hammerman
DIC Enterprises Inc.
3601 West Olive Avenue
Burbank, CA 91505
Andy Heyward, executive producer
ABC animated series

**Headline News
(a division of CNN)**
One CNN Center, P.O. Box
105366
Atlanta, GA 30348–5366
W. Thomas Johnson, president
*Syndicated world and national
news briefs*

Hollywood Pictures
500 South Buena Vista Street
Burbank, CA 91521
Richard Mestres, president
Movie production company

**Home Box Office, Inc.
(HBO)**
1100 Avenue of the Americas
New York, NY 10036
Michael Fuchs, chairman/CEO
Premium cable movie channel

**Imagine Films Entertainment,
Inc.**
1925 Century Park East, Suite
2300
Los Angeles, CA 90067
Brian Grazer, Ron Howard, co-
chairmen
Film production company

In Living Color
P.O. Box 900
Beverly Hills, CA 90213
Keenen Ivory Wayans, executive
producer
Fox Network comedy series

Jim Henson's Muppet Babies
Marvel Productions Ltd.

4640 Lankershim Boulevard,
Suite 600
North Hollywood, CA 91607
Joe Taritero, executive producer
CBS animated series

Kid 'N Play
Marvel Productions Ltd.
4640 Lankershim Boulevard,
Suite 600
North Hollywood, CA 91607
Joe Taritero, executive producer
NBC animated series

Life Goes On
Warner Brothers Television
4000 Warner Boulevard
Burbank, CA 91522
Michael Braverman, executive
producer
ABC series

Lifetime Television
34–12 36th Street
Astoria, NY 11106
Thomas Burchill, president
Cable network

Lorimar Television
300 Lorimar Plaza
Burbank, CA 91505
David Salzman, president
Television production company

MacGyver
Paramount Network Television
5555 Melrose Avenue
Hollywood, CA 90038
Stephen Downing, John Rich,
Henry Winkler, executive pro-
ducers
ABC series

Married . . . With Children
Columbia Pictures Television
4000 Warner Boulevard
Burbank, CA 91522
Ron Leavitt, Michael G. Moye, executive producers
Fox network series

MCA, Inc.
100 Universal City Plaza
Universal City, CA 91608
Lew R. Wasserman, chairman of the board/CEO
Television and film production company, the parent company of Universal Studios.

Mister Rogers' Neighborhood
WQED/Pittsburgh
4802 Fifth Avenue
Pittsburgh, PA 15213
Fred Rogers, executive producer
Long-running PBS series

Monday Night Football
ABC Sports
47 West 66th Street
New York, NY 10023
Jack O'Hara, executive producer

Mother Goose & Grimm
Film Roman
12020 Chandler Boulevard, #200
North Hollywood, CA 91607
Phil Roman, executive producer
CBS animated series

The Movie Channel
c/o Showtime Networks, Inc.
1633 Broadway
New York, NY 10019
Winston H. Cox, chairman/CEO
Premium cable movie channel

MTV Networks
1515 Broadway
New York, NY 10019
Thomas E. Freston, chairman/CEO
Music television cable network

NBC Entertainment
a division of National Broadcasting, Inc.
3000 West Alameda Avenue
Burbank, CA 91523
Brandon Tartikoff, chairman NBC Entertainment Group
Program division of NBC

NBC Television Network
a division of National Broadcasting Inc.
30 Rockefeller Plaza
New York, NY 10112
John Welch, Jr., chairman, NBC Inc.
Television network

Nickelodeon/Nick at Night
1633 Broadway
New York, NY 10019
Geraldine Laybourne, president
Cable channel for kids

Paramount Communications, Inc.
5555 Melrose Avenue
Hollywood, CA 90038
Martin S. Davis, chairman/CEO

Television and film production company

Parker Lewis Can't Lose
Columbia Pictures Television
4000 Warner Boulevard
Burbank, CA 91522
Clyde Phillips, executive producer

Fox network series

Perfect Strangers
Lorimar Television
300 South Lorimar Plaza
Burbank, CA 91505
Thomas L. Miller, Robert L. Boyett, William Bickley, Michael Warren, executive producers

ABC series

The Pirates of Dark Water
Hanna-Barbera Productions, Inc.
3400 Cahuenga Boulevard, West
Hollywood, CA 90068
David Kirschner, executive producer

ABC animated series

Prime Ticket Network
10000 Santa Monica Boulevard
Los Angeles, CA 90067–7007
John Severino, president

Sports cable network

Prostars
DIC Enterprises Inc.
3601 West Olive Avenue
Burbank, CA 91505
Andy Heward, executive producer

Animated series

Public Broadcasting Service
(PBS)—Executive Headquarters
1320 Braddock Place
Alexandria, VA 22314
Bruce Christensen, president/CEO

Viewer-supported noncommercial television network.

Rescue 911
Arnold Shapiro Productions
5800 Sunset Boulevard, Building 12
Hollywood, CA 90028
Arnold Shapiro, executive producer

CBS television series hosted by William Shatner.

Roseanne
The Carsey-Werner Company
4024 Radford Avenue, #3
Studio City, CA 91604
Marcy Carsey, Tom Werner, executive producers

ABC sitcom

Sesame Street
Children's Television Workshop
One Lincoln Plaza
New York, NY 10023
Dulcy Singer, executive producer

PBS series

Showtime Networks, Incorporated
1633 Broadway
New York, NY 10019
Winston H. Cox, chairman/CEO

Premium cable channel

The Silent Network

American Disability Network
1777 NE Loop 410, Suite 1401
San Antonio, TX 78212
Dr. Bill Nichols, president

Network for the deaf and hearing-impaired.

The Simpsons

20th Century Fox Television
P.O. Box 900
Beverly Hills, CA 90213
James L. Brooks, Matt Groening, Sam Simon, executive producers

Fox network animated series

Slimer & the Real Ghostbusters

DIC Enterprises Inc.
3601 West Olive Avenue
Burbank, CA 91505
Michael C. Gross, executive producer

ABC animated series

Sports Channel

1545 26th Street
Santa Monica, CA 90404–3554
Lynn Woodard, president

Cable premium sports channel

Square One TV

Children's Television Workshop
One Lincoln Plaza
New York, NY 10023
Jeffrey Nelson, executive producer

PBS series

Star Trek: The Next Generation

Paramount Network Television Productions
5555 Melrose Avenue
Hollywood, CA 90038
Rick Berman, Michael Piller, executive producers

Syndicated series

Super Mario 4

DIC Enterprises Inc.
3601 West Olive Avenue
Burbank, CA 91505
Andy Heyward, executive producer

NBC animated series

Superstation TBS

Turner Broadcasting, Incorporated
One CNN Center
P.O. Box 105366
Atlanta, GA 30348–5366
R. E. Turner, chairman of the board/president

Television superstation

Swamp Thing

DIC Enterprises Inc.
3601 West Olive Avenue
Burbank, CA 91505
Benjamin Melniker, executive producer

Live-action version of the comic book, shown on USA Network.

Teenage Mutant Ninja Turtles

Group W Productions
3801 Barham Boulevard
Los Angeles, CA 90068
Fred Wolf, supervising producer

Saturday morning cartoon version of the super-heroes

3-2-1 Contact Extra's
Children's Television Workshop
One Lincoln Plaza
New York, NY 10023
Anne MacLeod, executive producer
PBS series

Tiny Toon Adventures
Warner Brothers Animation, Inc.
15303 Ventura Boulevard, Suite 1100
Sherman Oaks, CA 91403
Steven Spielberg, executive producer
Syndicated animated series

Touchstone Pictures
500 South Buena Vista Street
Burbank, CA 91521
David Hoberman, president
Movie production company

Tri-Star Pictures
3400 Riverside Drive
Burbank, CA 91505
Mike Medavoy, chairman
Movie production company

Turner Network Television (TNT)
One CNN Center, P.O. Box 105336
Atlanta, Georgia 30348–5366
Scott Sassa, president, Turner Entertainment Networks
Television network

Twentieth Century Fox, Inc.
10201 West Pico Boulevard
Los Angeles, CA 90035
Barry Diller, chairman/CEO
Television and film production company

USA Network
1230 Avenue of the Americas
New York, NY 10020
Kay Koplovitz, president/CEO
Cable television network

Video Hits 1 (VH-1)
MTV Networks
1515 Broadway
New York, NY 10036
Edward A. Bennett, president
Music television cable network

Walt Disney Pictures
500 South Buena Vista Street
Burbank, CA 91521
David Hoberman, president
Movie production company

Wheel of Fortune
Merv Griffin Enterprises
9860 Wilshire Boulevard
Beverly Hills, CA 90210
Merv Griffin, executive producer
Game show

Where's Waldo
DIC Enterprises Inc.
3601 West Olive Avenue
Burbank, CA 91505
Andy Heyward, executive producer
CBS animated series

Who's the Boss?
Columbia Pictures Television
4000 Warner Boulevard
Burbank, CA 91522
Martin Cohan, Blake Hunter, Danny Kallis, executive producers
ABC series

Wishkid
DIC Enterprises Inc.
3601 Olive Avenue
Burbank, CA 91505
Andy Heyward, executive producer
NBC animated series

The Wonder Years
New World Television
1440 South Sepulveda Boulevard
Los Angeles, CA 90025
Bob Brush, executive producer
ABC sitcom

Yo, Yogi!
Hanna-Barbera Productions, Inc.
3400 Cahuenga Boulevard
Los Angeles, CA 90068
William Hanna, Joseph Barbera, executive producers
NBC animated series

The Young Riders
MGM/UA Television Productions
10000 West Washington Boulevard
Culver City, CA 90232
Scott Shepherd, executive producer
ABC western series

GET BUSY!

A list of clubs and organizations for kids of all ages. Topics include:

Agriculture/Farming/Animals
Animal Rights
Art and Writing
Book Clubs
Health
Hobbies/Games
Drama, Film, Television
Environment
Ethnic/Nationalist Groups
Exchange Students/Pen Pals

Fan Clubs
Leadership Clubs
Peace Groups
Politics
Religious Groups
Science
Scouting
Space/Flying
Sports (See also "Sports Fans" chapter)

Academy of Family Films and Family Television
334 West 54th Street
Los Angeles, CA 90037
Dr. Donald A. Reed, executive director

Membership includes students, teachers, librarians, and filmmakers, whose purpose is to improve the quality of motion pictures and television.

Academy of Model Aeronautics
1810 Samuel Morse Drive
Reston, VA 22090
Geoffrey Styles, director of public relations

Provides a magazine for model airplane builders and rock-eteers; also provides insurance for its members.

Action for Children's Television
20 University Road
Cambridge, MA 02138
Peggy Charren, president

Sponsors seminars and symposiums regarding television and children.

AFS International/Intercultural Programs
313 East 43rd Street
New York, NY 10017
Beryll Levinger, president

Promotes international exchange of high school students from over 60 countries.

Air Jordan Flight Club
P.O. Box 2300
Dept. SI
Portland, OR 97208–2300
Club for Michael Jordan fans.

American Academy of Achievement
P.O. Box 548
Malibu, CA 90265
Wayne R. Reynolds, executive director
Sponsors "Salute to Excellence" conference for 400 honor students.

American Boychoir Federation (also Federation Internationale des Choeurs des Enfants)
120 South Third Street
Connellsville, PA 15425
Rodolfo Torres, president, American Boychoir Federation
Ralph M. Cook, president, Federation Internationale
Association of 1,400 boy choirs throughout the US.

American Carpatho-Russian Youth
American Carpatho-Russian Orthodox Diocese
312 Garfield Street
Johnstown, PA 15906
Very Rev. John R. Fedornock, national spiritual advisor
A youth group for young people of the Carpatho-Russian Diocese.

American Checker Foundation
National Youth Program
1345 North Van Pelt Avenue
Los Angeles, CA 90063
Doyle Saucier, national youth director
Sponsors checkers tournaments in two youth divisions.

American Friends Service Committee Youth Programs
1501 Cherry Street
Philadelphia, PA 19102
Hilda Grauman, coordinator
Offers summer work camps and service opportunities in Mexico for young people.

American Indian Science and Engineering Society
1085 14th Street, Suite 1506
Boulder, CO 80302–7309
Norbert S. Hill, Jr., executive director
Merges appreciation of Indian cultural heritage with science and technology. Offers scholarships for older students.

American Junior Academy of Science
Biology Department
University of Richmond
Richmond, VA 23173
Dr. R. Dean Decker, director
Write to this organization to get more information on state and local clubs for kids interested in scientific investigation.

American Junior Hereford Association
P.O. Box 014059
Kansas City, MO 64101
Bonnie Coley, head, youth activities department
An agriculture and livestock association.

American Junior Paint Horse Association
American Paint Horse Association
P.O. Box 18519
Fort Worth, TX 76118
Rosemary Pittman, youth coordinator
An agriculture and livestock association.

American Junior Quarterhorse Association
P.O. Box 200
Amarillo, TX 79168
Julie Johnson, director of youth activities
Horsebreeder's association

American Junior Shorthorn Association
8288 Hascall Street
Omaha, NB 68124
Steve McGill, junior activities director
Livestock breeder's association

American Numismatic Association
818 North Cascade Avenue
Colorado Springs, CO 80903
James Taylor, education director

Robert Hoge, museum curator
Junior membership available to kids ages 11–17 interested in coin collecting.

American Rabbit Breeders Association
1925 South Main
P.O. Box 426
Bloomington, IL 61704
Glen C. Carr, secretary
Breeder's association

American Red Cross
Program and Services Department
17th and D Streets, NW
Washington, DC 20006
Susan B. Walter, youth associate
Organizes the Junior Red Cross, safety education, and recently has focused on AIDS education.

American Romanian Orthodox Youth
2522 Grey Tower Road
Jackson, MI 49201
Teva Reagle, national president
The youth group for the Romanian Orthodox church.

American Sokol Organization
6424 West Cermak Road
Berwyn, IL 60402
George C. Basta, president
An organization to promote the Czech culture, customs, and language.

American Student Council Association
National Association of Elementary School Principals
1516 Duke Street
Alexandria, VA 22314–3483
Margaret Evans, student services coordinator

An organization that helps elementary and middle schools participate in student governments.

American Theater Arts for Youth
1511 Walnut Street
Philadelphia, PA 19102
Laurie Wagman, executive director

Sponsors film and theater programs for kids.

American Zionist Youth Foundation
515 Park Avenue
New York, NY 10022
Ruth Kastner, executive director

A coordinating service agency for member organizations which provides programs for the purpose of bringing Jewish youth closer to Israel and Judaism.

Amigos de las Americas
5618 Star Lane
Houston, TX 77057
Cedie Sencion, director of recruiting

A non-profit, international organization that promotes leadership development in Latin America.

Amnesty International
Attn: Children's Urgent Action Network
322 Eighth Avenue
New York, NY 10001

An independent, worldwide movement working impartially for the release of all prisoners of conscience, fair and prompt trial for political prisoners, and an end to torture and executions.

Anchor Clubs
Pilot Club International
Pilot International Building
P.O. Box 4844
Macon, GA 31213
Dorothy Lewis, executive administrator

These clubs promote leadership development in kids through service to school and community.

Anti-Defamation League of B'nai B'rith
823 United Nations Plaza
New York, NY 10017
Dr. Frances M. Sonnenschein, director, National Education Department

Dedicated to the ideals of democracy and the fight against bigotry and discrimination.

Armenian Church Youth Organization of America
Juvenile Division—Armenian
  Church of America
630 Second Avenue
New York, NY 10016
Douglas Tashjian, executive secretary

The youth program of the Armenian church.

Aspira Association, Inc.
1112 16th Street, NW, Suite 340
Washington, DC 20036
Dr. Janice Petrovich, national executive director

An Hispanic youth group that encourages education and leadership development.

Association of American Youth of Ukrainian Descent
4004 Roanoke Circle
Minneapolis, MN 55422
Anatoly Lysyj, MD, president

A youth group for kids ages 7 and up of Ukrainian birth or descent.

Awana Clubs International
One East Bode Road
Streamwood, IL 60107
Dr. Art Rorheim, president

A Christian youth group for kids ages 3 through high school.

Baha'i National Youth Committee
Baha'i National Center
Wilmette, IL 60091

Jenni Mileham, manager, youth
  desk

For youth of the Baha'i faith, ages 12 and up.

Beginning Readers Program
Grolier Enterprises
Sherman Turnpike
Danbury, CT 06816
Steve Fishman, senior vice-president

A book club for very young kids, featuring hardcover books from Random House.

Berean Youth Fellowship
P.O. Box 100
Oregon, IL 61601
Kent Ross, director

The youth program of the Church of God of the Abrahamic Faith.

Betar
38 East 23rd Street
New York, NY 10010
Eli Cohen, director

A Zionist Jewish organization for youth ages 13–18.

Big Brothers/Big Sisters of America
230 North 13th Street
Philadelphia, PA 19108
Thomas McKenna, national executive director

Formed through the merger of Big Brother and Big Sister organizations, this group matches volunteer adults with kids from single-parent homes.

B'nai B'rith Youth Organization
1640 Rhode Island Avenue, NW
Washington, DC 20036
Dr. Sidney M. Clearfield, international director

An international Jewish youth organization serving teens.

Bnei Akiva of North America
25 West 26th Street, 4th Floor
New York, NY 10010
Noah Slomovitz, director

A religious Zionist youth movement with educational programs that promote Jewish culture.

Boy Scouts of America
1325 Walnut Hill Lane
Irving, TX 75038-3096
Ben H. Love, executive director

Boys Clubs of America
771 First Avenue
New York, NY 10017
John L. Burns, president

Boys' and Girls' Brigades of America
P.O. Box 9863
Baltimore, MD 21284
Joseph Sauthoff, president

A program of Bible and missions training for kids ages 6–18.

Byelorussian–American Youth Organization
P.O. Box 1123
New Brunswick, NJ 08903
George Azarko, president

Promotes the Byelorussian culture among descendants in the US. Also sponsors scholarship programs for graduate studies in Eastern European area studies.

Cadet Commanderies, Knights of St. John
Knights of St. John Supreme Commandery
6517 Charles Avenue
Parma, OH 44129
Brig. Gen. Salvatore LaBianca, supreme secretary

Membership is comprised of Catholic young men, ages 8–16.

Camp Fire, Inc.
4601 Madison Avenue
Kansas City, MO 64112
Margaret Preska, president

Camping and public service organization for girls.

Campus Crusade for Christ International
Arrowhead Springs
San Bernardino, CA 92414
Dr. Bill Bright, founder and president

An evangelical student outreach program.

The Caravan Program
Nazarene Youth International, The Church of the Nazarene
6401 The Paseo
Kansas City, MO 64131

Kathy Hughes, Caravan coordinator

Gary Siveright, director

This program offers scouting-type activities for kids from preschool to grade six.

Catholic Big Brothers of New York, Inc.
1011 First Avenue
New York, NY 10022
Merrie Teil-Green, spokesperson

Matches boys ages 7–15 with adult friends.

Cherokee Nation Youth Leadership Program
P.O. Box 948
Tahlequah, OK 74465
Diane Kelley, director, Department of Youth Leadership

A program to develop the potential of Cherokee youth.

Child Evangelism Fellowship
P.O. Box 348
Warrenton, MO 63383
Alan George, president

International organization that seeks to reach children through Bible classes, camps, rallies, and other programs.

Children of the Confederacy
United Daughters of the Confederacy
328 North Boulevard
Richmond, VA 23220–4057
Marion H. Giannasi, office manager

Organization for boys and girls under 21 who are direct descendants of Confederates.

Children of the Republic of Texas
The Daughters of the Republic of Texas
5758 Balcones Drive, Suite 201
Austin, TX 78731
Carolyn Weed, CRT director

For descendants of people who resided in or fought for Texas before 1846.

Children of War
Religious Task Force
85 South Oxford Street
Brooklyn, NY 11217
Judith Thompson, program director

Group promoting international peace among kids ages 13–18, including refugee youth.

Children's Action for Animals
American Humane Education Society
350 South Huntington Avenue
Boston, MA 02130
Judith Golden, director

Club- or classroom-based program to aid kids in their understanding of animal life.

Children's Art Foundation
Box 83
Santa Cruz, CA 95063
William Rubel, executive director

Operates a children's art museum and sponsors afterschool art and writing programs. Also operates a research archive of children's writing and art.

Children's Braille Book Club
National Braille Press Inc.
88 St. Stephen Street
Boston, MA 02115
Diane L. Croft, marketing manager

Book club for the blind

Children's Campaign for Nuclear Disarmament
14 Everit Street
New Haven, CT 06511
Lisa Berger, president

Completely youth-run organization dedicated to ending the arms race.

Children's Express
245 Seventh Avenue
New York, NY 10001
Robert Clampitt, president

News service reported by children 13 and under who are trained and led by teen assistant editors. Has news bureaus in the US and overseas.

Children's Special Edition/ Urgent Action
Amnesty International
P.O. Box 1270
Nederland, CO 80466
Ellen Moore, assistant program coordinator

Letter-writing program for grades 4–8, where kids write letters on behalf of other children who need help.

Christian Service Brigade
P.O. Box 150
Wheaton, IL 60189
C. Samuel Gray, president

Evangelical Christian program for boys ages 6–18.

The Church of Jesus Christ of Latter-Day Saints
The Primary Association, The Young Men, The Young Women
76 North Main Street
Salt Lake City, UT 84150
Michaelene Grassli, president, The Primary Association
Ardeth G. Kapp, president, The Young Women
Vaughn J. Featherstone, president, The Young Men

Youth organizations of the Church of Jesus Christ of Latter-Day Saints (Mormons).

Church Ministries Department
General Conference of Seventh-Day Adventists, North American Division
12501 Old Columbia Pike
Silver Spring, MD 20904–1608
Norm O. Middag, spokesperson

Seventh-Day Adventists youth groups for a variety of ages.

Civil Air Patrol
Building 714
Maxwell Air Force Base, AL
    36112–5570
Director, Office of Public Affairs

Kids, grade school through college, can be cadets and receive training in air search and rescue work, meteorology, and aviation.

Clowns of America, Inc.
P.O. Box 570
Lake Jackson, TX 77566–0570
Dennis Phelps, president

Organization for everyone interested in clowning.

Club Del Libro
AIMS International Books, Inc.
3216 Montana Avenue
Cincinnati, OH 45211
Denise Crowell, marketing manager

Book club for Spanish language books.

Coalition for Christian Outreach
6740 Fifth Avenue
Pittsburgh, PA 15208
Rev. Robert R. Long, president

Interdenominational evangelistic student ministry working in Pennsylvania, Ohio, and West Virginia.

Co-Ette Club
2020 West Chicago Boulevard
Detroit, MI 48206

Mary-Agnes Miller Davis, MSW, executive sponsor

Organization for leadership training and community service for black girls.

Columbian Squires
Knights of Columbus Supreme Council
One Columbus Plaza
New Haven, CT 06507
Harvey G. Bacque, director, Fraternal Services

Program for boys ages 12–18 sponsored by the Knights of Columbus that seeks to develop leadership skills.

Constellation of Junior Stars, Inc.
P.O. Box 55
Greenwood Lake, NY 10925
Edna T. Salvidge, president of the Grand Council

Youth division of the Masons.

Council on International Educational Exchange
205 East 42nd Street
New York, NY 10017
Jack Egle, President/Executive Director

Non-profit organization that administers volunteer service programs for American and international students.

D.A.R.E.

(Drug Abuse Resistance Education)
150 North Los Angeles Street, Suite 439
Los Angeles, CA 90012

Anti-drug clubs sponsored by local police enforcement organizations.

Degree of Anona/Degree of Hiawatha
Great Council of the United States/Improved Order of Red Men

4007 West Waco Drive, P.O. Box 683
Waco, TX 76703
Robert E. Davis, great chief of records

Youth programs of the Order of Red Men, a fraternal organization for American Indians.

Degree of Honor Protective Association Junior Clubs

325 Cedar Street
St. Paul, MN 55101
Elayne E. Blazick, national president

Clubs promote civic responsibility through educational, social, and service activities.

Disney's Wonderful World of Reading

Grolier Enterprises
Sherman Turnpike
Danbury, CT 06816
Steve Fishman, senior vice-president

Book club for young children, featuring Disney stories.

Drum Corps, International

P.O. Box 548
Lombard, IL 60148
Donald Pescone, director

Federation of school and community drum corps.

Earthwatch

680 Mount Auburn Street
Box 403N
Watertown, MA 02272
Brian A. Rosborough, president

Organization that studies the earth and its inhabitants with an eye toward protecting them.

Elim Fellowship, Inc.—Youth Department
Christian Youth Aflame, Teen World Outreach, Christ's Helpers in Parental Strife

7245 College Street
Lima, NY 14485
Tony Martorana, youth director

Pentecostal youth groups

Elsa Clubs of America

P.O. Box 4572
North Hollywood, CA 91607
A. Peter Rasmussen, Jr., general manager

Clubs involve young people in the care and protection of our natural world.

Ezrah Youth Movement

Poale Agudath Israel of America
4405 13th Avenue

Brooklyn, NY 11219

Rabbi Sholom Rephun, director

Zionist movement for youth ages 9–25 that seeks to educate members in Jewish and Torah values and lifestyle.

Federated Russian Orthodox Clubs

10 Downs Drive

Wilkes Barre, PA 18705

Peter Khoudie, Jr., president

Youth group for members of the Russian Orthodox church.

Fellowship of Christian Athletes

8701 Leeds Road

Kansas City, MO 64129

Richard F. Abel, president

Evangelical program open to Christian athletes in junior and senior high schools.

Fellowship of Reconciliation

P.O. Box 271

Nyack, NY 10960

Jo Becker, coordinator, Youth Activities

Conducts the Children's Creative Response to Conflict Program, dedicated to promoting nonviolent responses to conflict.

4-H Youth Development

Cooperative Extension Service, US Department of Agriculture

Washington, DC 20250

Dr. Leah Hoopfer, deputy administrator

For kids ages 9–19 interested in agriculture, natural resources, and the American family.

Free Church Student Fellowship

Evangelical Free Church

1515 East 66th Street

Minneapolis, MN 55423

Reverend Steve Hudson, associate director of Church Ministries

Organization for youth in grades 7–12 that encourages "a personal relationship to Christ."

Free Methodist Church of North America

Christian Life Club, Young Teen Program, Senior Teen Program

901 College Avenue

Winona Lake, IN 46590

Michael B. Merrill, director of Youth Ministries

Christian Life Clubs for elementary through high school kids.

FRONTLASH

815 16th Street, NW

Washington, DC 20006

Joel Klaverkamp, executive director

Youth support group for the AFL-CIO, whose purpose is to teach kids about labor unions.

Future Farmers of America

National FFA Center

5632 Mt. Vernon Highway, P.O. Box 15160

Alexandria, VA 22309

Larry D. Case, national advisor

For kids interested in vocational agriculture and agribusiness, or just farming.

Future Homemakers of America
1910 Association Drive
Reston, VA 22091
Alan T. Rains, Jr., executive director

For young men and women interested in home economics and consumer education.

Gavel Club Program
Toastmasters International
2200 North Grand Avenue
Santa Ana, CA 92711
Greg Giesen, manager, Membership and Club Extension

Promotes excellence in public speaking and parliamentary procedure.

Girl Scouts of the USA
830 Third Avenue
New York, NY 10022
Frances Hesselbein, executive director

Programs available for girls ages 5–17.

Girls in Action/Acteens
Women's Missionary Union/ Auxiliary to the Southern Baptist Convention
P.O. Box 830010
Birmingham, AL 35238–0010
Ethel McIndoo, consultant, Girls in Action
Marty Solomon, consultant, Acteens

These groups were founded in 1817 to teach missions education.

Girls Clubs of America
30 East 33rd Street
New York, NY 10016
Margaret Gates, executive director

200 clubs throughout the US for girls ages 6–18.

Grace Contrino Abrams Peace Education Foundation
3550 Biscayne Boulevard, Suite 400
Miami, FL 33137
Warren S. Hoskins, executive director

Teaches kids to "fight fair," and also teaches kids to try to mediate their disputes.

Greek Orthodox Young Adult League
27–09 Crescent Street
Astoria, NY 11102
Father Angelo Gavalas, national youth director

Youth program for members of the Greek Orthodox Church.

Habonim-Dror Labor Zionist Youth Movement
27 West 20th Street, 9th Floor
New York, NY 10011
Charles Buxbaum, executive director

Zionist youth movement that provides spiritual, cultural, and physical training to increase appreciation of the Jewish heritage.

Hashomer Hatzair
150 Fifth Avenue
New York, NY 10011
Chaim Brum, director

Jewish organization that promotes traditional kibbutz values and lifestyle.

Hermann Sons Youth Chapters
Order of the Sons of Hermann in
  Texas
P.O. Box 1941
San Antonio, TX 78297
Allan Preuss, youth coordinator

Fraternal benefit organization, originally for people of German descent. The group now has a broader base and sponsors youth groups, mostly in Texas.

Histadruth Ivrith of America
1841 Broadway
New York, NY 10023
Dr. Aviva Barzel, executive vice-
  president

Organization for kids dedicated to the advancement of Hebrew language and culture.

The Holstein Junior Program
The Holstein Association of
  America
1 Holstein Place
P.O. Box 808
Brattleboro, VT 05301
Neil Hammerschmidt, director,
  Field Services

Livestock breeder's association

Hugh O'Brian Youth Foundation
10880 Wilshire Boulevard, Suite
  900
Los Angeles, CA 90024
John M. Claerhout, president and
  CEO

Sponsors leadership seminars for outstanding students.

Indian Youth of America
P.O. Box 2786
Sioux City, IA 51106
Patricia Trudell Gordon, execu-
  tive director

Youth group dedicated to improving the lives of American Indian kids; builds self-esteem and pride in the Native American culture.

Inner City Outings
Sierra Club
730 Polk Street
San Francisco, CA 94109
Debra Asher, Inner City Outings
  coordinator

Community outreach program of the Sierra Club, this program provides wilderness adventures for inner-city kids.

Interact
Rotary International
1560 Sherman Avenue, One Rotary Center
Evanston, IL 60201
Rebecca Fritz, program coordinator, Community Service
  and Youth Activities

Program for kids ages 14–18 that aims to develop leadership, integrity, and helpfulness to others.

International Arabian Horse Youth Association
P.O. Box 33696
Denver, CO 80233
Jean Gilligan, president

Horse breeder's association

International Christian Youth Exchange
134 West 26th Street
New York, NY 10001
Andrea Lee Spencer, director of Outbound Programs

Sponsors international experiences for young people.

International Friendship League
55 Mount Vernon Street
Boston, MA 02108
Margaret MacDonough, executive director

Links American students with pen pals in 127 countries.

International Good Templars Youth Fellowship
International Organization of Good Templars
National Council of the USA, National Office & Museum
2926 Cedar Avenue
Minneapolis, MN 55407
Anna L. Danielson, national director of youth work

Organization that promotes total drug and alcohol abstinence for youth.

International Junior Brangus Breeders Association
International Brangus Breeders Association
P.O. Box 696020
San Antonio, TX 78269–6020
Dawn Kent, director of programs

Livestock breeder's association

International Order of Job's Daughters
Supreme Guardian Council
233 West 6th Street
Papillion, NE 68046
Susan M. Goolsby, executive manager

Youth group affiliated with the Masons for girls ages 11–20.

International Order of the King's Daughters and Sons
1750 Taft Avenue
Evansville, IN 47714
Mrs. Philip Bruner, international director, Junior Department

Interdenominational and international organization whose youth department seeks to develop the spiritual life and stimulate Christian activities.

International Pentecostal Holiness Church
General Christian Education, Department C
Women's Ministries, Department C

P.O. Box 12609
Oklahoma City, OK 73157
Reverend Doyle G. Marley, director of General Christian Education
Doris Moore, director of Women's Ministries

Encompasses several Pentecostal youth programs.

International Society of Christian Endeavor
1221 East Broad Street
P.O. Box 1110
Columbus, OH 43216
Reverend David G. Jackson, general secretary

One of the oldest societies for young people, founded in 1881. Membership includes members 6–adult.

International Thespian Society
3368 Central Parkway
Cincinnati, OH 45225
Ronald L. Longstreth, executive director

Honor society for junior and senior high school students who are members of drama groups.

International Wizard of Oz Club, Inc.
220 North 11th Street
Escanaba, MI 49829
Fred Meyer, secretary

Club for Wizard of Oz enthusiasts of all ages.

Jewish Publication Society
1930 Chestnut Street

Philadelphia, PA 19103
Sheila F. Segal, editor

Book club for school-age kids.

Jr. Auxiliary
Supreme Ladies' Auxiliary
2648 Queenston Road
Cleveland, OH 44118
Isabel Shea, supreme president

Organization for girls ages 8–16 which promotes interest in the adult women's organization.

Junior Achievement
45 East Clubhouse Drive
Colorado Springs, CO 80906
Karl Flemke, president

Has programs designed for grades 4–12 that provide the basics of the private enterprise system. Kids get to develop and operate their own small businesses.

Junior American Citizens Committee
Daughters of the American Revolution
1776 D Street, NW
Washington, DC 20006
Mrs. John M. Ivancevich, national chairwoman

Membership is open to all kids, ages 6 and up. Purpose is to develop informed citizens.

Junior Civitan International
Civitan International
P.O. Box 130744
Birmingham, AL 35213–0744
Louis M. Stephens, staff director

Junior and senior high school group that seeks to promote good citizenship, support good government, and encourage respect for the law.

Junior Cultural Federation of America/Junior Tamburitzans Croatian Fraternal Union of America
100 Delaney Drive
Pittsburgh, PA 15235
Bernard M. Luketich, national president

Groups are open to all kids with an interest in Croatian culture.

Junior Daughters of the King
435 Peachtree Street, NE
Atlanta, GA 30365
Mrs. Christopher Allaire, national chairwoman

Organization of lay members of the Episcopal church, for girls ages 8–20.

Junior Daughters of Peter Claver/Junior Knights of Peter Claver
1825 Orleans Avenue
New Orleans, LA 70116
Earl D. Harvey, director general (Jr. Knights)
Anetta Wilson, national counselor (Jr. Daughters)

Catholic youth organizations for kids 7–17, primarily for community service. Peter Claver was a Jesuit who aided victims of the African slave trade.

Junior Deputy Sheriffs' Program
National Sheriffs' Program
1450 Duke Street
Alexandria, VA 22314
Betsy Cantrell, coordinator of Junior Deputy Program

Trains kids in emergency preparedness, law enforcement, and local government.

Junior Division, Ancient Order of Hibernians in America
31 Logan Street
Auburn, NY 13021
Thomas McNabb, national secretary

Youth group for kids ages 9–16 that promotes Irish history and culture.

Junior Exchange Clubs
National Exchange Club
3050 Central Avenue
Toledo, OH 43606
James A. Schnoering, executive vice-president

Promotes responsible American citizenship, service to the community and sponsors the "One Nation Under God Program" and the National Youth of the Year Award.

Junior Fire Marshal Program
Herman Marketing, Inc.
1400 North Price Road
St. Louis, MO 63132–2308
Freda Cook, account manager

Program for grades K–3 conducted by local fire departments on fire safety and fire prevention.

Junior Girls Units

Ladies Auxiliary to the Veterans of Foreign Wars
34th and Broadway
Kansas City, MO 64111
Glenn Grossman, national secretary-treasurer

Community service and service to hospitalized veterans. Membership is open to girls ages 6–16 who are the daughters of war veterans.

Junior Great Books

Great Books Foundation
40 East Huron Street
Chicago, IL 60611
John Riley, national training coordinator

Sponsors reading and discussion of "great books" for elementary through high school students.

Junior Guardian Angels

Guardian Angels
982 East 89th Street
Brooklyn, NY 11236
Curtis Sliwa, founder

Guardian Angels is an organization of trained volunteers who seek to deter crime through unarmed street patrols. The Junior Angel program does community service.

Junior International Federation of Catholic Alumni

St. Mary's Academy
2404 Russell Road
Alexandria, VA 22301
Sister Roberta, contact person

Organization for any girls who attend Catholic high school.

Junior Literary Guild

245 Park Avenue
New York, NY 10167
Marjorie Jones, director

Book club for school-age children.

Junior Lodge, Independent Order of Odd Fellows

Sovereign Grand Lodge Office
422 Trade Street
Winston-Salem, NC 27101
Norman Gleason, sovereign grand secretary

The Odd Fellows club for kids. The Odd Fellows are a fraternal lodge.

Junior Members, American Legion Auxiliary

777 North Meridan Street
Indianapolis, IN 46204
Miriam Junge, national secretary

Community service organization for girls under 18 who are the daughters of war veterans.

Junior Optimist Octagon International

Optimist International
4494 Lindell Boulevard
St. Louis, MO 63108

Ruby Blair, director

Civic service organizations for junior and senior high school students.

Junior Order of the Serb National Federation
3 Gateway Center
6F1 South
Pittsburgh, PA 15222
Robert Rade Stone, president

Promotes Serbian language and culture to kids under 16.

Junior Philatelists of America
P.O. Box 701010
San Antonio, TX 78270–1010
David Flack, president

Helps young stamp collectors organize their collections and learn about their hobby. Enclose self-addressed stamped envelope for more information.

Junior Service Clubs/Teen Clubs
Modern Woodmen of America
Mississippi River at 17th Street
Rock Island, IL 61201
Rita Johnson, assistant manager, youth division, Fraternal Department

Youth groups that promote patriotism, community service, and teach parliamentary procedure.

Junior Sons of America
Patriotic Order, Sons of America
1547 Pratt Street
Philadelphia, PA 19124

Harvey Stoehr, executive secretary

Organization for kids ages 1–18 devoted to the study of the Constitution and an appreciation of freedom.

Junior Statesmen of America
Junior Statesmen Foundation
650 Bair Island Road, Suite 201
Redwood City, CA 94063
Richard Prosser, executive director

Also known as the Junior State, this organization helps prepare young leaders for active participation in government.

Junior Ukrainian Orthodox League of the USA
One St. John's Parkway
Johnson City, NY 13790
Father Myron Oryhon, spiritual adviser

Youth organization for members of the Ukrainian church.

JWB
15 East 26th Street
New York, NY 10010
Arthur Roman, executive vice-president

Association of Jewish Community Centers.

Key Club International
Kiwanis International
3636 Woodview Terrace
Indianapolis, IN 46268
David A. Wohler, administrator

Organization that promotes service to schools and community, with leadership training.

Keyette International
Ki-Wives International
1421 Kalmia Road, NW
Washington, DC 20012
Ruth Wolford, chairman
Service organization for girls.

Khmer Youth Leadership Council
179 East Robie
St. Paul, MN 55117
Susan Tabbert, program coordinator
Program for kids 14 and up who are of Khmer descent. Seeks to rebuild Cambodian families.

Kids in Nature's Defense— National Association for the Advancement of Humane and Environmental Education
P.O. Box 362
East Haddam, CT 06423
Patty Finch, executive director
Sponsors the Helping Hands for Pets program, to teach kids to be responsible and humane.

Knights of Lithuania—Juniors
45 Windsor Drive
Oakbrook, IL 60521
Sabina Henson, vice-president
Lithuanian youth group for kids under 18. Promotes the Lithuanian culture.

League of Tarcisians of the Sacred Heart
P.O. Box 111
3 Adams Street
Fairhaven, MA 02719
Father Alphonsus Mitchell, SS, CC, national director
Catholic youth organization for elementary through high school age kids.

League of Ukrainian Catholic Youth
St. Peter and Paul Church
2280 West 7th Street
Parma, OH 44113
Monsignor John E. Stevensky, spiritual director
Groups for young people of the Ukrainian Catholic Church which foster interest in their religious and cultural heritage.

Lithuanian Catholic Federation Ateitis
7235 South Sacramento
Chicago, IL 60629
Juozas Polikaitis, president
Federation of Lithuanian cultural and religious youth organizations.

Little Friends for Peace
4405 29th Street
Mount Ranier, MD 20712
Mary Joan Park, director
Peacemaking skills education program for young children.

Luther League Federation

Association of Free Lutheran Congregations
3110 East Medicine Lake Boulevard
Minneapolis, MN 55441
Reverend Dennis Gray, Youth Resources Director

Program in Lutheran congregations for kids 9 to young adults.

MADRE

Women's Peace Network
121 West 27th Street
New York, NY 10001
Lilliana Cortes, Children's Program Coordinator

Seeks to foster friendships between children in the United States and Central America.

Magical Youths International

61551 Bremen Highway
Mishawaka, IN 46544
Steve Kelley, advisor

Correspondence organization for kids interested in magic. Some major cities have their own chapters. Also publishes Top Hat.

Maids of Athena

Daughters of Penelope
1707 L Street, NW, Suite 200
Washington, DC 20036
Helen Pappas, executive director

Youth organization to promote high ethical standards and appreciation of Greek culture.

Masada of the Zionist Organization of America

4 East 34th Street
New York, NY 10016
Kobi Greitser, director

Zionist organization open to all Jewish youth 13–22, which promotes Jewish culture.

Mensa

2626 East 14th Street
Brooklyn, NY 11235
Margot Seitelman, executive director

Adult organization that sponsors activities on a local level for kids who have scored in the upper 2 percent on intelligence tests.

Missionettes

Assemblies of God
1445 Boonville Avenue
Springfield, MO 65802
Linda Upton, National Auxiliaries Coordinator

Advancement program of Bible memorization, missions education, and other aspects of religious education for kids ages 3 and up.

Mobilization for Survival Youth Task Force

11 Garden Street
Cambridge, MA 02138
Loreto Ruiz-Barra, youth coordinator

Organization that strives to abolish nuclear weapons, nuclear power, military intervention, and reverse the arms race.

NAD Youth Programs
National Association for the Deaf
445 North Pennsylvania Avenue, Suite 804
Indianapolis, IN 46204
David J. Schultz, Youth Program Coordinator

Programs and assistance for deaf students.

National Association of Student Councils
National Association of Secondary School Principals
1904 Association Drive
Reston, VA 22091
Dale D. Hawley, director, Division of Student Activities

Federation of student councils in secondary schools.

National Association of Youth Clubs
5808 16th Street NW
Washington, DC 20011
Carole A. Early, headquarters secretary

Community-based clubs for boys and girls ages 8–18 under the sponsorship of the National Association of Colored Women's Clubs.

National Audubon Society
National Education Office
R.R. #1, Box 171
Sharon, CT 06069
Marshall Case, vice-president for Education

Sponsors "Audubon Adventures" program, and the Audubon Expedition Institutes for kids.

National Beta Club
P.O. Box 730
151 West Lee Street
Spartanburg, SC 29304
George W. Lockamy, executive director

Academic, leadership, and service organization for students grades 5–12.

National Catholic Forensic League
21 Nancy Road
Milford, MA 01757
Richard Gaudette, secretary-treasurer

Speech and debate league for students in parochial, private, and public high schools.

National Christ Child Society, Inc.
5101 Wisconsin Avenue, NW
Washington, DC 20016
Mrs. Ronald W. Chamblee, president

All-volunteer, nonprofit Catholic organization that provides multiple services to children and youth, regardless of race or creed.

National Council of Young Israel
3 West 16th Street
New York, NY 10011
Richard Stareshefsky, director
*Promotes traditional Judaism
and education in the heritage
and culture of the Jewish people
for kids from first grade to college.*

National Energy Foundation
5160 Wiley Post Way, Suite 200
Salt Lake City, UT 84116
Edward A. Dalton, EdD, president and CEO
*Sponsors the Student Exposi-
tion on Energy Resources and
the Youth Wants to Know program.*

**National Federation for Catholic
Youth Ministry**
3900-A Hairwood Road, NE
Washington, DC 20017
James A. Knowles, executive di-
rector
*Federation of Catholic youth or-
ganizations.*

National Forensic League
671 Fond du Lac
Ripon, WI 54971
James Copeland, executive secretary
*Honor society which promotes
debate, discussion, and public
speaking.*

National Gardening Association
180 Flynn Avenue
Burlington, VT 05401

Tim Parsons, Education Programs Director
*Helps people become success-
ful gardeners. Publishes* The
Youth Garden Book.

**National Grange Junior/
National Grange Youth and
Young Adults**
1616 H Street, NW
Washington, DC 20006
Wayne and Peggy Miller, National
Junior leaders
Bernie and Helen Shoemaker,
National Youth leaders
*Youth programs of the National
Grange, an agricultural frater-
nity.*

**National Hampshire Junior As-
sociation**
6748 North Forestwood Parkway
Peoria, IL 60615
Rick Maloney, executive secretary
Breeder's association

National Indian Youth Council
318 Elm Street, SE
Albuquerque, NM 87102
Cheryl J. Mann, executive direc-
tor
*Provides services to American
Indian youth.*

**National Indian Youth Leader-
ship Project**
101 South Clark Street
Gallup, NM 87301

McClellan Hall, founder and director

Created to provide opportunities to American Indian youth.

National Junior Angus Association
American Angus Association
3201 Frederick Boulevard
St. Joseph, MO 64501
Mark Wyble, director of Junior Activities

Livestock breeder's association.

National Junior Honor Society
1904 Association Drive
Reston, VA 22091
Dale D. Hawley, contact

For students who excel in scholarship, leadership, and character.

National Junior Horticultural Association
441 East Pine Street
Fremont, MI 49412
Jan Hoffman, executive secretary

Program for kids interested in horticulture. No membership fees or dues.

National Junior Polled Hereford Council
c/o Youth Department American Polled Hereford Association
4700 East 63rd Street
Kansas City, MO 64130
Annette Forst, director of Youth Activities

Livestock breeder's association

National Junior Santa Gertrudis Association
Santa Gertrudis Breeders International
P.O. Box 1257
Kingsville, TX 78364
Kenneth Ellis, director of youth activities and publicity

Agriculture and breeding association

National Organization, Sons of Union Veterans of the Civil War
411 Barlett Street
Lansing, MI 48915
James T. Lyons, national secretary-treasurer

Membership is open to boys who are direct descendants of Union Civil War veterans.

National Society of the Children of the American Revolution
1776 D Street, NW
Washington, DC 20006
Ms. Stiles A. Wilkins, administrator

For lineal descendants, from birth to age 22, of patriots of the American Revolution.

National TEC Conference
3501 State Street
Omaha, NE 68112
Sister Joy Connealy, ND, executive director

TEC is an acronym for "Teens Encounter Christ," a Catholic organization.

National Teen Age Republican Headquarters

8587 B Sudley Road
P.O. Box 1896
Manassas, VA 22110
Barbara Wells, national director

Educates teens in principles of free enterprise, constitutional government, and patriotism. Some areas also have Sub-Teen Age Republicans.

National Tots and Teens, Inc.

P.O. Box 1517
Washington, DC 20013–1517
James Jackson, national president

Group for families with kids ages 3–18 that fosters strong family life. Also does fundraising for the United Negro College Fund.

National Traditionalist Caucus

P.O. Box 971, G.P.O.
New York, NY 10116
Don Rosenberg, national chairman

Program for junior and senior high school students that stresses patriotism, conservative values, anti-Communism, and free enterprise.

National Youth Ministry Organization

United Methodist Church
Box 840
Nashville, TN 37202

Jack B. Harrison, executive director

Youth advocacy agency for the United Methodist Church.

The Navigators

6516 North University, #901
Peoria, IL 61604
Jim Rinella, high school ministry director

International, non-denominational organization that tries to help people grow through Bible studies and one-on-one help.

NCJW Junior Council

National Council of Jewish Women
53 West 23rd Street
New York, NY 10010
Dadie Perlov, executive director

Junior section of the National Council of Jewish Women.

North American Association of Ventriloquists

800 West Littleton Boulevard
P.O. Box 420
Littleton, CO 80160
Clinton Detweiler, president

Assists and encourages budding ventriloquists with product and technical information.

North American Federation of Temple Youth

Union of American Hebrew Congregations (Reform)
838 Fifth Avenue
New York, NY 10021

Rabbi Ramie Arian, director

Youth groups for members of Reform congregations.

North American Junior Limousin Foundation
P.O. Box 16767
Denver, CO 80216
Wayne Vanderwert, director

Agriculture and breeder's association.

Open Door Student Exchange
250 Fulton Avenue
P.O. Box 71
Hempstead, NY 11551
Howard Bertenthal, president

International student exchange program.

Order of the Builders for Boys
Route 1, Box 1246
Wampum, PA 16157
Robert V. Beard, Supreme Master Builder

Program for boys ages 11–21, sponsored by the Masons.

Partners in Peacemaking
The People Care Center
120 Finderne Avenue
Bridgewater, NJ 08807
Marsha Howard, executive director

Peacemaking program for elementary school kids.

Peace Child Foundation
3977 Chain Bridge Road
Fairfax, VA 22030
David R. Woollcombe, president

Promotes joint international exchange projects in the performing arts on the theme of peace and global survival. Projects are for children of the US and Russia.

Pentecostal Young People's Association
Pentecostal Church of God, Inc.
Box 705
Joplin, MO 64802
Dr. Phil L. Redding, general PYPA president

Programs for kids of all ages and young adults.

Pioneer Clubs
Pioneer Ministries, Inc.
P.O. Box 788
27 West 130 St. Charles Road
Wheaton, IL 60189
Virginia Patterson, president

International activity-based program for Christian youth enrolled through their churches.

The Planetary Society
65 North Catalina Avenue
Pasadena, CA 91106
Carl Sagan, president

Has programs for science students who are interested in planetary exploration.

PLAST, Ukrainian Youth Organization
144 Second Avenue
New York, NY 10003
Ihor R. Sochan, president

Coed organization based on scouting principles; its primary purpose is to perpetuate the Ukrainian cultural heritage.

Polish National Alliance of the United States of North America Youth Programs

6100 North Cicero Avenue
Chicago, IL 60646
Anthony S. Piwowarczyk, vice-president and chairman of Sports and Youth Commission

Fraternal organization sponsoring youth programs that promote the Polish language and culture.

Presbyterian Church (USA) Youth Club

100 Witherspoon Street
Louisville, KY 40202–1396
Rodger Nishioka, national director, Presbyterian Youth Ministry

Umbrella organization for all the youth groups in the Presbyterian Church (USA).

Puppeteers of America

Five Cricklewood Path
Pasadena, CA 91107
Paul Eide, president

Holds national puppetry festivals, workshops, and exhibits for amateur and professional puppeteers.

Pythian Sunshine Girls

Pythian Sisters
P.O. Box 87
Pine Village, IN 47975
Becky Blimm, Supreme Royal Princess

Club for girls 8–20 who are relatives of Knights of Pythias or Pythian Sisters.

Royal Ambassadors

Brotherhood Commission of the Southern Baptist Convention
1548 Poplar Avenue
Memphis, TN 38104
Reverend Russell Griffin, director, Children and Youth Division

Baptist educational program for boys.

Royal Rangers

Assemblies of God
1445 Boonville Avenue
Springfield, MO 65802
Johnnie Barnes, national commander

Program for boys ages 5–17 that seeks to promote physical, spiritual, mental, and social growth.

Salvation Army National Headquarters

Girl Guards, Adventure Corps
799 Bloomfield Avenue
Verona, NJ 07044
Colonel Harold Shoults, chief secretary

Outreach programs of the Salvation Army for kids of all ages.

Save Our Streams
The Izaak Walton League of America, National Office
1401 Wilson Boulevard, Level B
Arlington, VA 22209
Karen Firehock, coordinator
Citizen action program for kids and youth groups. Groups adopt a stream and commit to caring for it year-round.

School Projectionist Club of America
Box 707
State College, PA 16804
Philip Monnino, executive director
Supports student projectionist clubs and publishes guides for use and repair of equipment. For information, send a SASE (legal size).

School Safety Patrols
American Automobile Association
1000 AAA Drive
Heathrow, FL 32745
Dean Childs, director, Traffic Safety Services
Organization for kids in grades 5 and 6 in the US and 30 foreign countries. Activities vary among the local clubs.

Skylarks/Oriole Girls/O-Teens
Reorganized Church of Jesus Christ of Latter-Day Saints
Box 1059, The Auditorium
Independence, MO 64051
Jerry Ashby, youth director
Scouting-type program for girls ages 8–18.

Slovak Catholic Sokol
205 Madison Street
P.O. Box 899
Passaic, NJ 07055
Tibor T. Kovalovsky, Supreme Secretary
Youth group for American Catholics of Slovak descent. Sponsors sports and also offers scholarships.

Slovak Gymnastic Union of the USA
276 Prospect Street
P.O. Box 189
East Orange, NJ 07019
John Sopoci, executive secretary
Slovak fraternal benefit organization that promotes gymnastics.

Sons of the American Legion
P.O. Box 1055
Indianapolis, IN 46206
John W. Kerestan, contact
Community service organization for the sons of war veterans.

Sons of Norway
Sons of Norway Youth Club, Unge Venner, Sons of Norway USA Cup
1455 West Lake Street
Minneapolis, MN 55408
Orlyn A. Kringstad, chief fraternal officer

Youth groups for ages 12–19, also sponsors a soccer tournament.

Sons of Pericles
Order of Ahepa
1707 L Street, NW, Suite 200
Washington, DC 20036
Greg Kalamaras, supreme president, Sons of Pericles

Promotes family life and a love and understanding of American and Hellenic cultures.

Sons of the Veterans of Foreign Wars
VFW Building, 12th Floor
34th and Broadway
Kansas City, MO 64111
Gordon R. Thorson, director of Youth Activities

Membership is open to boys under 18 whose fathers or grandfathers are eligible for membership in the VFW. Promotes rapport between fathers and sons.

Space Camp/Space Academy
The Space & Rocket Center
One Tranquility Base
Huntsville, AL 35807

Instead of swimming and singing by the campfire, be an astronaut for the summer.

**Spartacus Youth League
c/o Spartacus Youth Publications**
P.O. Box 3118
Church Street Station

New York, NY 10960
Alison Spencer, secretary

Committed to building a revolutionary Socialist movement of working-class youth.

Star Blazers
4505 Silver Hollow Drive
Corpus Christi, TX 78413
Diane Weiner, director

Space-age educational organization for boys and girls age 7 and older.

Student Action Corps for Animals
P.O. Box 15588
Washington, DC 20003
Rosa Feldman, director

Group works with students who want to participate in the animal rights movement, principally those students who oppose vivisection.

The Student Conservation Association, Inc.
P.O. Box 550
Charlestown, NH 03603
Scott D. Izzo, president

Sponsors volunteer work groups in national parks and forests for teenagers.

Students and Youth Against Racism
P.O. Box 1819, Madison Square Station
New York, NY 10159
Jelayne Miles, spokesperson

National student organization dedicated to fighting racism, lesbian and gay bigotry, and sexism.

Success with Youth

Christian Education Publishers
Box 261129
San Diego, CA 92126
Arthur L. Miley, publisher

Non-denominational club-based ministry that works with kids ages 3–18.

Teen Association of Model Railroading

Lone Eagle Payne
1028 Whaley Road, RD #4
New Carlisle, OH 45344
Stan Ujka, president

Promotes building and operating of model railroads.

Texas and Southwestern Cattle Raisers Association

1301 West 7th Street
Fort Worth, TX 76102
Don C. King, secretary and general manager

Livestock breeder's association

Theta Rho Girls' Club International Association of Rebekah Assemblies, IOOF

422 Trade Street, Suite R
Winston-Salem, NC 27101
Janet Simmonds, international secretary

Youth group of the Rebekah Assemblies for girls ages 10–21.

Touch America Program

US Forest Service
P.O. Box 96090
Washington, DC 20090
Don Hansen, director, Human Resource Programs

Program to teach kids about natural resources through volunteer conservation projects on public lands.

Tzivos Hashem—Lubavitch

332 Kingston Avenue
Brooklyn, NY 11213
Rabbi Yerachmiel Benjaminson, executive director

Jewish youth organization for boys under 13 and girls under 12.

Ukrainian American Association, Inc.

136 Second Avenue
P.O. Box 211
New York, NY 10003
Maria Platka, secretary

Group for kids ages 5 and up of Ukrainian descent. Programs include folk dancing, music, and sports teams.

United Calvinist Youth

Calvinettes, Cadets, Young Calvinist Federation
P.O. Box 7259, 1333 Alger Street, SE
Grand Rapids, MI 49510
Joanne Ilbrink, director, Calvinettes

Richard Broene, director, Cadets
Brian Bosscher, director, Young
Calvinist Federation

*Christian scouting-type activities
for kids of all ages.*

Victory Leaders Band
The Church of God of Prophecy
P.O. Box 2910
Cleveland, TN 37320–2910
William M. Wilson, general secretary

*Youth ministry arm of the
Church of God of Prophecy.*

Weekly Reader Children's Book Club
Field Publications
245 Long Hill Road
Middletown, CT 06457
Betsy Isele, executive editor

*Book club for elementary school
kids, featuring books from major juvenile publishers.*

Western Young Buddhist League
Buddhist Churches of America
1710 Octavia Street
San Francisco, CA 94109
Eido Tai Shimano, Roshi (Abbot)

*Coordinates the activities of
young Buddhists of the Jodo
Shinshu denomination.*

Women's Department, Polish Roman Catholic Union of America
984 North Milwaukee Avenue
Chicago, IL 60622

Regina Ocwieja, vice-president,
head of Women's Department

*Women's department sponsors
Polish language classes, dance,
and choral groups for kids.*

Woodcraft Rangers
2111 Park Grove Avenue
Los Angeles, CA 90007
James Van Hoven, executive director

Scouting-type program

Woodmen Rangers
Woodmen of the World
1700 Farnam Street
Omaha, NE 68102
Larry R. Wegener, manager, National Youth Activities

*Scouting-type program for kids
ages 8–15 sponsored by a fraternal organization.*

World Federalist Association
P.O. Box 15250
Washington, DC 20003
Anthony Allen, youth director

*Supports the United Nations
with 70 youth and adult chapters.*

World Vision
919 West Huntington Drive
Monrovia, CA 91016
Robert A. Seiple, president

*International Christian relief and
development agency that primarily sponsors children.*

YMCA of the USA
101 North Wacker Drive
Chicago, IL 60606
Solon B. Cousins, executive director

Various programs available for children and adults.

Young Actors Guild
125 South 4th Street
Connellsville, PA 15425
Aaron White, president

Membership organization that protects the interests of young professional performers.

Young Americans for Freedom
380 Maple Avenue West
Vienna, VA 22180
Thomas C. Lizardo, executive director

Nation's oldest and largest nonpartisan conservative political youth organization.

Young Astronaut Program
1211 Connecticut Avenue, NW, Suite 800
Washington, DC 20036
T. Wendell Butler, executive director

For elementary and junior high students interested in science, math, and technology.

Young Communist League of the United States of America
235 West 23rd Street, 6th Floor
New York, NY 10011
John Bachtell, chairman

Organization that provides kids ages 14 and up with opportunities to learn about socialism.

Young Democrats of America
c/o Democratic National Committee
430 South Capitol Street, SE
Washington, DC 20003
Kathy McGough, spokesperson

Youth organization for the Democratic Party.

Young Entomologists Society
International Headquarters
1915 Peggy Place
Lansing, MI 48910
Gary Dunn, executive director

Society for kids interested in the study of insects.

Young Judaea/Haschachar
50 West 58th Street
New York, NY 10019
Irv Widaen, national director

Largest of the Zionist youth organizations, with programs for kids in grades 4–12.

Young Life
720 West Monument Street
P.O. Box 520
Colorado Springs, CO 80901
Douglas Burleigh, president

Non-denominational, community-based program that seeks to introduce young people to the gospel of Christ.

Young Marines of the Marine Corps League, Inc.
35237 Lana Lane
Sterling Heights, MI 48077
Byron Haase, national director
Physical fitness and "character building" program for boys and girls ages 8–17.

Young Religious Unitarian Universalists
Unitarian Universalist Association
25 Beacon Street
Boston, MA 02108
Meg Riley, director of Youth Programs
Program for kids that encourages learning, worship, fellowship, and social action.

Young Republican National Federation
310 First Street, SE
Washington, DC 20003
Terry Campo, national chairman
Youth organization of the Republican Party.

Young Socialist Alliance
191 Seventh Avenue, 2nd Floor
New York, NY 10011
Greg McCarten, national organization secretary
Promotes socialist ideas.

Young Vikings of the Danish Brotherhood in America
3717 Harney Street
Omaha, NE 68131
Pamela K. Dorau, director, Fraternal Services
Youth groups that promote Danish language and culture.

Young Women's Christian Association of the United States of America (YWCA)
726 Broadway
New York, NY 10003
Gwendolyn Calvert Baker, executive director
Programs in health, fitness, and education available for all ages.

Youth Against War and Facism
46 West 21st Street
New York, NY 10010
Kathy Durkin, corresponding secretary
Group that opposes war, imperialism, racism, and discrimination. Also advocates prison reform.

Youth and Government
YMCA of the USA
101 North Wacker Drive
Chicago, IL 60606
Tom Massey, program associate
Program where kids participate in model state legislatures and the annual Youth Governors Conference.

Youth Section of the Democratic Socialists of America
15 Dutch Street, Suite 500
New York, NY 10038
Dinah Leventhal, youth organizer

Works to protect the rights of women, workers, and minorities, and also promotes the idea of an equitable distribution of the nation's wealth.

Zioneers/Zion's League
Reorganized Church of Jesus Christ of Latter-Day Saints

Box 1059, The Auditorium
Independence, MO 64051
Jerry Ashby, youth director

Youth groups organized through individual congregations.

IT *IS* YOUR BUSINESS

Fast food, clothes, games, toys, etc.

A & W Restaurants
17197 North Laurel Park Drive, Suite 500
Livonia, MI 48152
E. Dale Mulder, CEO/chairman of the board

Fast-food chain

A. C. Nielsen Company
Nielsen Plaza
Northbrook, IL 60062
N. Eugene Harden, president

Television ratings company

ACA Joe, Inc.
148 Townsend Street
San Francisco, CA 94107
Alice Wany Lam, CEO/chairman of the board

Chain of clothing stores

Adidas USA, Inc.
15 Independence Boulevard
Warren, NJ 07060
Ann Occi, director of creative services and public relations

Manufacturer of sportswear and equipment

Admiration Toy Company Inc.
60 McLean Avenue
Yonkers, NY 10705
S. Newman, president

Manufacturer of dolls and stuffed toys

After the Stork, Inc.
1501 12th Street, NW
Albuquerque, NM 87104
Alan Stopper, president

Children's clothing-store chain

Airwalk
Division of Items International
2042 Corte Del Nogal, Suite A
Carlsbad, CA 92009
William Mann, president

Importer of general sports equipment, athletic shoes, etc. Specializes in skateboarding shoes.

Alfa Candy Corporation
P.O. Box 344
New York, NY 10034
George Atstaedter, president

Manufactures "healthy" candy

All Star Sporting Goods
Subsidiary of Ampac Enterprises, Inc.
1 Main Street
P.O. Box 1356
Shirley, MA 01464
David J. Holden, president
Manufactures baseball equipment

Alpo Petfoods, Inc.
P.O. Box 2187
Lehigh Valley, PA 18001
Franklin Krum, CEO
Pet food manufacturer

AMC Entertainment Inc.
106 West 14th Street
Kansas City, MO 64105
Stanley H. Durwood, CEO
Movie theater chain

American Ball Manufacturing Corporation
1225 Tappan Circle
Carrollton, TX 75006
William V. Brown, president
Sporting goods and athletic equipment manufacturer

American Blimp Corporation
1900 N.E. 25th Avenue, Suite 5
Hillsboro, OR 97124
James R. Thiele, president
Blimp manufacturer

American Bread Company
P.O. Box 100390
Nashville, TN 37210
Charles K. Evers, CEO
Cookies and crackers manufacturer

American Chewing Gum Inc.
Eagle and Lawrence Road
Havertown, PA 19083
Edward L. Fenimore, president
Chewing gum manufacturer

American Chicle Group
810 Main Street
Cambridge, MA 02139
Donald R. Eberhart, manager
Candy and confectionery manufacturer

American Desk Manufacturing Company
P.O. Box 6107
Temple, TX 76503
Paul W. Kerr, president
Manufacturer of school desks

American Greetings Corporation
10500 American Road
Cleveland, OH 44144
Morry Weiss, CEO/president
Greeting card manufacturer

American Sammy Corporation
2421 205th Street, Suite D–104
Torrance, CA 90501
Manufactures software for electronic games.

American Seating Company
901 Broadway
Grand Rapids, MI 49504
Albert H. Meyer, president, Arch
    Products Group

Manufactures stadium and arena seating.

Apple Computer Inc.
20525 Mariami Avenue
Cupertino, CA 95014
John Sculley, CEO/chairman of the board

Manufactures Apple and Macintosh computer hardware and software.

APSCO Enterprises
50th Street and First Avenue
Building Number 57
Brooklyn, NY 11232
Rudy DiPietro, president

Manufactures, distributes, and imports official caps, pennants and T-shirts for: NBA, NCAA, NHL, major league baseball and NFL.

Arena U.S.A., Inc.
Subsidiary of Adidas
28 Engelhard Drive
Cranbury, NJ 08512
Peter Tannenbaum, vice-president of merchandising

Manufactures sports apparel. Brands include Flyback, Freeback, and Superflyback.

Ask a Silly Question
P.O. Box 1950
Hollywood, CA 90078
Kathleen Conner, president

Research and information service

Astroturf Industries Inc.
Subsidiary of Balsam Corporation
809 Kenner Street
Dalton, GA 30720
E. M. Milner, president

Manufactures AstroTurf.

Atari Corporation
1196 Borregas Avenue
Sunnyvale, CA 94086
Sam Tramiel, CEO/president

Video game manufacturer

ATEC
115 Post Street
Santa Cruz, CA 95060
Jack Shepard, chief executive officer

Manufactures, distributes, and exports baseball and softball equipment. Brands include Casey, Grand Slam USA, Hummer and Tuffy.

Austin Athletic Equipment Corporation
705 Bedford Avenue, Box 423
Bellmore, NY 11710
Jonathan Austin, president

Manufactures and distributes sports equipment. Brands include: All American, AMF, Curvemaster, Jayfro, Kwik-goal, Marcy, Playworld, etc.

AVIA
Subsidiary of Reebok International, Ltd.
16160 SW Upper Boones Ferry Road

Portland, OR 97224
William Dragon, Jr., president/
CEO

Manufactures sports shoes.

**Bachrach Rasin Sporting
Goods, Inc.**
802 Gleneagles Court
Towson, MD 21204
Frederick W. Whitridge, president

*Imports and distributes all kinds
of sporting goods and equipment.*

Baskin-Robbins USA Company
P.O. Box 1200
Glendale, CA 91209
Jim Earnhardt, president

"31 flavors" ice-cream company

Bausch & Lomb
42 East Avenue
P.O. Box 743
Rochester, NY 14603–0743
Norman D. Salik, vice-president
public relations/promotions,
Eyewear Division

*Manufactures sunglasses.
Brands include Ray-Ban, Way-
farer, and Wings.*

**Bell Bicycle, Inc.
Subsidiary of Echelon Sports
Corporation**
15301 Shoemaker Avenue
Norwalk, CA 90650
Phil Mathews, president/CEO

*Wholesaler of bicycle helmets.
Brands include: Lil Bell Shell,
Pro Plus, BMX, SR-1, SR-2,*

*Stratos, Tourlite, V-1 Pro, and
Windjammer.*

**Ben and Jerry's Homemade Ice
Cream**
P.O. Box 240
Waterbury, VT 05676
Ben Cohn, Jerry Greenfield,
owners

Bic Pen Corporation
500 Bic Drive
Milford, CT 06460
Bruno Bich, president

Ball-point pen manufacturer

**Bike Athletic Company
Subsidiary of Kazmaier Inter-
national**
P.O. Box 666
Knoxville, TN 37901
James R. Corbett, president

*Manufactures and distributes
sports clothing and protective
equipment.*

Binney & Smith, Inc.
P.O. Box 431
Easton, PA 18044
Richard Guren, CEO

Manufactures Crayola crayons.

B.M.X. Products
1250 Avenida a Caso, Suite H
Camarillo, CA 93010
Skip Hess, president

*Manufactures bicycles, including
the Mongoose.*

Buffalo Inc.
North 724 Madelia
Spokane, WA 99202
Peter Lindstrom, president
*Manufacturers of Fruit of the
Loom products*

Burger King
17777 Old Cutler Road
Miami, FL 33157
Barry J. Gibbons, CEO
Fast-food chain

Buster Brown Apparel
2001 Wheeler Avenue
Chattanooga, TN 37406
Kent C. Robinson, CEO
Children's clothing company

Cadaco Incorporated
4300 West 47th Street
Chicago, IL 60632
Wayman Wittman, president
Manufactures board games.

Carl's Jr.
1200 North Harbor Boulevard
Anaheim, CA 92801
Carl N. Karcher, Jr., chairman
Fast-food chain

Catalina, Inc.
**Subsidiary of Kayser/Roth In-
corporated**
6040 Bandini Boulevard
Los Angeles, CA 90040
John E. Watte, Jr., president
*Manufactures gymnastic ap-
parel, water sports apparel, and
bathing suits.*

Champion Products Inc.
**Subsidiary of SaraLee Corpora-
tion**
P.O. Box 850
3141 Monroe Avenue
Rochester, NY 14603
Roger Holland, president/CEO
Manufactures sports apparel.

Church's Fried Chicken
1333 South Clearview Parkway
Jefferson, LA 70121
Alvin C. Copeland, chairman
Fast-food chain

Cineplex Odeon Corporation
1925 Century Park East, Suite
300
Los Angeles, CA 90067
E. Leo Kolber, chairman of the
board
Movie theater chain

Coca-Cola Enterprises Inc.
1 Coca-Cola Plaza, NW
Atlanta, GA 30313
Brian G. Dyson, CEO/president
Soft drink company

Cole of California
**Subsidiary of Wickes Com-
panies**
1615 Fruitland Avenue
Los Angeles, CA 90058
George Green, president
*Manufactures gymnastic ap-
parel, water sports apparel, and
swimsuits.*

Converse Inc.
1 Fordham Road
North Reading, MA 01864
Richard B. Loynd, chairman

Manufactures athletic shoes. Brands include: All Star, Chris Evert, Chuck Taylor, Converse, Jimmy Connors, Phaeton, Road Star, and Weapons.

Create-a-Book
The Book Factory
c/o Hotel Del Coronado
1500 Orange Avenue
Coronado, CA 92118

This company will personalize books for kids.

Cycles Peugeot, USA, Incorporated
Subsidiary of Cycles Peugeot
555 Gotham Parkway
Carlstadt, NJ 07072
Alexander Sacerdoti, executive vice-president

Manufacturer, distributor, and importer of bicycles, equipment and apparel.

Dairy Queen
P.O. Box 35286
Minneapolis, MN 55435
Michael P. Sullivan, chief executive officer

Fast-food chain

Dakin Inc.
P.O. Box 7746
San Francisco, CA 94120
Harold A. Nizamian, president

Stuffed-animal manufacturer

Diadora America
6529 South 216th, Building E
Kent, WA 98032
Galliano Mondin, chief operating officer

Manufactures athletic shoes. Brands include: Boris Becker, Bjorn Borg, James Donaldson, and Pat Cash.

Domino's Pizza Incorporated
P.O. Box 997
Ann Arbor, MI 48106
Tom Monaghan, president

Fast-food chain

Dreyer's Grand Ice Cream Inc.
5929 College Avenue
Oakland, CA 94618
T. Gary Rogers, CEO/chairman of the board

Ice-cream manufacturer

Edwards Theatres Circuit, Inc.
300 Newport Center Drive
Newport Beach, CA 92660
James Edwards, Sr., chairman

Movie theater chain

Electronic Arts
2755 Campus Drive
San Mateo, CA 94403
Larry Probst, president/CEO

Creates and manufactures the software for video games. Loves to get letters from kids about what they think of the games.

E. S. Originals
20 West 33rd Street
New York, NY 10001
Ellis Safdeye, president

*Manufactures athletic shoes.
Brands include: Coppertone,
Easy Going, Flintstones, Harley
Davidson, New York Street, Ac-
tion, Regent, Safety Lights,
Sasson, Sergio Valente, Voit.*

**Everlast Sporting Goods Manu-
facturing Company**
750 East 132nd Street
Bronx, NY 10454
Ben Nadorf, president

Sporting goods company

Fanatic Limited
Robin Hill Corporate Park
Route 22
Patterson, NY 12563
Peter Juen, president

*Distributor of Sailboards, acces-
sories, and water sports
apparel.*

F.A.O. Schwarz
767 Fifth Avenue
New York, NY 10153
John Eyler, president

Great toy store

Federal Express Corporation
2990 Airway
Memphis, TN 38194
Frederick W. Smith, chairman

*When you send away for things,
they are frequently shipped by
this company instead of mailed.*

Fisher-Price
636 Girard Avenue
East Aurora, NY 14052
Ronald Jackson, chairman/CEO

Toy manufacturer

Foster Grant Corporation
Foster Grant Plaza
Leominster, MA 01453
Richard Wright, president

*Manufactures eyewear, sun-
glasses, and protective eyewear.*

Frito-Lay
7701 Legacy Drive
Plano, TX 75024
Michael H. Jordan, president

Junk food company

GAP Incorporated
One Harrison
San Francisco, CA 94105
Donald G. Fisher, CEO

Clothing store chain

Gapkids
Gap Stores Incorporated
900 Cherry Avenue
San Bruno, CA 94066
Donald G. Fisher, chairman of
    the board

Kid's division of The Gap

General Mills
9200 Wayzatta Boulevard
Minneapolis, MN 55440
H. B. Atwater, Jr., chief executive
    officer

Food manufacturer

Ghirardelli Chocolate Company
111 139th Street
San Leandro, CA 94578
Dennis DeDomenico, chairman
Candy company

Guess Inc.
1444 South Alameda Street
Los Angeles, CA 90021
Maurice Marziano, president
Clothing manufacturer

Häagen-Dazs Company Inc.
Glen Pointe
Teaneck, NJ 07666
Michael L. Bailey, president
Ice-cream manufacturer

Hallmark Cards
2501 McGee Trafficway, Suite 419580
Kansas City, MO 64141
Irvine O. Hockaday, Jr., chief executive officer
Greeting card company

Harley Davidson Motor Company
3700 West Juneau Avenue
Milwaukee, WI 53208
Vaughn Le Roy Beals, Jr., president
Last American motorcycle company

Hasbro Inc.
1027 Newport Avenue
Pawtucket, RI 02862
Alan G. Hassenfeld, CEO/chairman of the board
Toy and game manufacturer

Hershey Foods
100 Mansion Road
Hershey, PA 17033
R. A. Zimmerman, chief executive officer
Chocolate manufacturer

Hudson Soft
400 Oyster Point Boulevard, Suite 515
South San Francisco, CA 94080
Electronic game software manufacturer

Huffy Corporation
P.O. Box 1204
Miamisburg, OH 45401
Harry A. Shaw III, president
Bicycle, bicycle accessory, and basketball manufacturer

IBM
(International Business Machines)
Old Orchard Road
Anorak, NY 10504
John Fellow Akers, president
Personal computer manufacturer

Jack-in-the-Box Restaurants
9330 Balboa Avenue
San Diego, CA 92112
Jack W. Goodall, Jr., chairman
Fast food chain

Keebler Company
1 Hollow Tree Lane
Elmhurst, IL 60126
Thomas M. Garvin, CEO/
president
*Sells cookies and crackers
baked by elves.*

K-Mart Corporation
3100 West Big Beaver
Troy, MI 48084
Joseph E. Antonini, chief operat-
ing officer
Department store chain

Kenner Products
1014 Vine Street
Cincinnati, OH 45202
David Mauer, president
Toy and game manufacturer

Kentucky Fried Chicken
P.O. Box 32070
Louisville, KY 40232
Richard P. Mayer, chairman
Fast food company

Levi Strauss
1155 Battery Street
San Francisco, CA 94111
Robert D. Haas, president
Jeans manufacturer.

Lewis Galoob Toys Inc.
500 Forbes Boulevard
South San Francisco, CA 94080
David Galoob, chairman/
president/CEO
*Toy manufacturer, maker of
Micro Minies*

Mattel
5150 Rosecrans Avenue
Hawthorne, CA 90250
Thomas J. Kalinske, president
Toy company

McDonald's Corporation
One McDonald Plaza
Oak Brook, IL 60521
Fred L. Turner, CEO
Fast-food chain

Milton Bradley Company
443 Shaker Road
East Longmeadow, MA 01028
George R. Ditamassi, president
Game manufacturer

M&M/Mars
High Street
Hackettstown, NJ 07840
Howard Walker, president
Candy company

Mrs. Field's Cookies
P.O. Box 680370
Park City, UT 84068
Debbie Fields, founder
Cookie company

Nestlé Food Corporation
100 Mahattanville Road
Purchase, NY 10577
C. A. MacDonald, president
Candy company

Nike
3900 SW Murray Boulevard
Beaverton, OR 97005
Philip H. Knight, chairman

Athletic shoe manufacturer

Nintendo
4820 150th Avenue, NE
Redmond, WA 98052
Hiroshi Yamauchi, president

Video game company. Manufactures and sells the machines that the games are played on, as well as some of the games themselves, such as Super Mario. Other games are licensed.

Oscar Mayer
P.O. Box 7188
Madison, WI 53707
James W. McVey, chief executive officer

Hot dog company

Parker Brothers
50 Dunham Road
Beverly, MA 01915
John Moore, president

Toy and game manufacturer

Pepsico
Anderson Hill Road
Purchase, NY 10577
D. Wayne Calloway, chief executive officer

Soft drink company

Playskool Inc.
110 Pitney Road
Lancaster, PA 17602
S. Erman, director

Toy manufacturer

Pressman Toy Corporation
200 Fifth Avenue, Suite 1052
New York, NY 10010
James R. Pressman, president

Toy manufacturer

RJR Nabisco Inc.
9 West 57th Street, 48th Floor
New York, NY 10019
Louis V. Gerstner, Jr., CEO/ chairman of the board

Cookies, crackers, nuts, and snack food manufacturer

Sara Lee Corporation
3 First National Plaza
Chicago, IL 60602
John H. Bryan, Jr., chief executive officer

Goodies manufacturer

Sega, Inc.
(Sega-Genesis)
573 Forbes Boulevard
South San Francisco, CA 94080
Thomas Kalinske, president

Software and hardware manufacturer of video games. Also licenses other companies to create software for Sega hardware.

7-Eleven
(Southland Corporation)
2828 North Haskell Avenue
Dallas, TX 75221
Jere W. Thompson, chief executive officer

Convenience store chain

Seven-Up Company
8144 Walnut Hill Lane
Dallas, TX 75231
John R. Albers, chief executive officer

Soft drink company

Swensens
P.O. Box 9008
Andover, MA 01810
Richard Smith, chairman

Ice-cream store chain

Taco Bell Corporation
17901 Von Karman
Irvine, CA 92714
John E. Martin, president

Fast-food chain

Tender Treasures
3706 Ocean View Boulevard
Montrose, CA 91020
Bonnie Beck, owner

Children's clothing store

Tonka Corporation
6000 Clearwater Drive
Minnetonka, MN 55343
Stephen G. Shank, chief executive officer

Toy company, manufactures famous trucks and games.

Tootsie Roll
7401 Cicero Avenue
Chicago, IL 60629
M. J. Gordon, president

Candy company

Toy Manufacturers of America, Inc.
200 Fifth Avenue
New York, NY 10010
Walter Armatys, executive director

Association of 250 toy manufacturers and importers. Also has toy-testing labs. If you have a complaint that a member company won't handle, write to the association!

Toys "Я" Us
395 West Passaic Street
Rochelle Park, NJ 07662
Charles Lazarus, chief executive officer

Toy store chain

Tyco Toys, Inc.
6000 Midlantic Drive
Mt. Laurel, NJ 08054
Richard E. Grey, president/ chairman/CEO

Game manufacturer

Warner Brothers Collections
Dept. TS
P.O. Box 60049
Tampa, FL 33660–0049

Mail order for Warner Brothers T-shirts, jackets, etc. Includes Looney Tunes characters.

Wendy's
4288 West Dublin Granville Road
Dublin, OH 43017
R. David Thomas, founder

Fast-food chain

Wm. Wrigley Jr. Company
410 North Michigan Avenue
Chicago, IL 60611
William Wrigley, CEO/president
Chewing gum manufacturer

Wrangler
P.O. Box 21488
Greensboro, NC 27420
Mackey McDonald, president
Jeans/clothing manufacturer

LET'S READ AND EXPLORE

Magazines, comic books, publishers, and museums

Action Comics
DC Comics, Inc.
355 Lexington Avenue
New York, NY 10017
Julius Schwartz, editor
Comic book

Alpha Flight
New World Entertainment/
   Marvel
387 Park Avenue South
New York, NY 10016
Stan Lee, publisher
Comic book

Amazing Heroes
Fantagraphics Books, Inc.
7563 Lake City Way
Seattle, WA 98115
Gary Groth, publisher
*Magazine of news and reviews
for comic book fans*

Amazing Spider Man
New World Entertainment/
   Marvel
387 Park Avenue South
New York, NY 10016
Stan Lee, publisher
Classic super-hero comic book

American Bible Society
1865 Broadway
New York, NY 10023
James Wood, president
*Publishes dictionaries, Bibles,
and spiritual texts.*

American College Testing Program
P.O. Box 168
Iowa City, IA 52243
Richard L. Ferguson, president
Designs achievement tests.

American Library Association
50 East Huron Street
Chicago, IL 60611
Herbert Bloom, editor
*Books published are primarily
for teachers and librarians, with
an emphasis on children's literature and library media skills.*

Angelfood
Meetinghouse Road
Walpole, NH 03608
Caroline M. Myss, editor-in-chief
   and children's editor
*Publishes books for pre-school
to grade 6, specializing in fic-*

tion, human potential, and psychology.

Animal Kingdom
New York Zoological Society
Zoological Park, 185 Street and
   Southern Boulevard
Bronx, NY 10460
Eugene J. Walter, Jr., editor
*Magazine that publishes articles
on ecology and wildlife*

Ann Arbor Hands-on Museum
219 East Huron
Ann Arbor, MI 48104
Cynthia Yao, director/curator
Museum where kids are encouraged to touch

Archie Comics
Archie Comic Publications, Inc.
325 Fayette Avenue
Mamaroneck, NY 10543
John L. Goldwater, publisher
Comic book

Arizona Museum for Youth
35 North Robson
Mesa, AZ 85201
Barbara Meyerson, director/
   curator

Art & Man
Scholastic Inc.
730 Broadway
New York, NY 10003
Richard Robinson, publisher
*Contains features for children
on art projects and art history.*

Arte Público Press
4800 Calhoun, #429 AH
Houston, TX 77004
Julian Olivares, editor-in-chief
*Publishes books for pre-school
to adults, specializes in American Hispanic authors.*

Asia Resource Center
Box 15275
Washington, DC 20003
Don Luce, director
*Publishes books on Asia for
K–4.*

**Association on American Indian
Affairs**
245 Fifth Avenue
New York, NY 10016
Alphonso Ortiz, president
*Provides information packets for
students and teachers.*

Association for Childhood Education International
11141 Georgia Avenue, Suite
   200
Wheaton, MD 20902
Lucy Prete Martin, editor
*Publishes books on a variety of
subjects for children.*

Avengers
New World Entertainment/
   Marvel
387 Park Avenue South
New York, NY 10016
Stan Lee, publisher
Comic book

Awani Press
Box 881
Fredericksburg, TX 78624
Frances C. Hubbard, children's
editor

Publishes books for K–6 and adults. Has a special interest in Native Americans.

Baha'i Publishing Trust
415 Linden Avenue
Wilmette, IL 60091
Betty J. Fisher, children's editor

Publishes books for K–12; specializes in nonsexist education, plus books for the reading disabled and blind.

Ball-Stick-Bird Publications, Inc.
Box 592
Stony Brook, NY 11790
Renee Fuller, children's editor

Publishes books for the mentally disabled, reading disabled, and bilingual students.

Barbie Magazine
Lorimar Publishing Group
300 Madison Avenue
New York, NY 10017
Karen Harrison, editor

A lifestyle and fashion magazine for girls, based on the Barbie doll.

Barron's Educational Series
113 Crossways Park Drive
Woodbury, NY 11797
Barbara Tchabovsky, children's
editor

Publishes a wide range of books for children and teenagers.

Baseball Card News
Baseball Cards
700 East State Street
Iola, WI 54990
Bob Lemke, publisher

Baseball Card News publishes information on collectibles, and card show listings. Baseball cards list current prices.

Batman
DC Comics Inc.
355 Lexington Avenue
New York, NY 10017
Julius Schwartz, editor

Super-hero comic book

Beaufort Books
Division of Kampmann and Company
Nine East 40th Street
New York, NY 10016
Susan Suffes, editor-in-chief

Publishes fiction and self-help for teenagers.

Bellwood Press
Box 605
Evanston, IL 60204-0605
Betty J. Fisher, editor

Publishes books for children on nonracist, nonsexist, and intercultural education.

Bethany House Publishers
6820 Auto Club Road
Minneapolis, MN 55438

Carol A. Johnson, editor-in-chief

Publishes books for children and adults on Christianity.

Better Baby Press
8801 Stenton Avenue
Philadelphia, PA 19118
Mary Ellen Cooper, editor-in-chief

Publishes books for children on a variety of subjects.

The Big Bopper
Laufer Publishing Company
3500 West Olive Avenue, Suite 850
Burbank, CA 91505
Julie Laufer, editor

Fan magazine

Biology Bulletin Monthly
General Learning Corporation
3500 Western Avenue
Highland Park, IL 60035
Laura Ruekberg, executive editor

Publishes children's features on biology and current events in science.

Birch Tree Group Ltd.
Box 2072
Princeton, NJ 08540
Ken Guilmartin, children's editor

Publishes material on music education.

Board of Jewish Education of Greater New York
426 West 58th Street
New York, NY 10019

Chaim Cohenson, children's editor

Publishes books on Israel, Jewish history, and culture and other related subjects for children and adults.

Bookmakers Guild, Inc.
1430 Florida Avenue, Suite 202
Longmount, CO 80501
Normandi Ellis, editor-in-chief

Publishes books for children on health, consumer education, the environment, etc.

Bop
Laufer Publishing Company
3500 West Olive Avenue, Suite 850
Burbank, CA 91505
Julie Laufer, editor

Fan magazine

Boys' Life
Boy Scouts of America
1325 Walnut Hill Lane
Irving, TX 75062
William B. McMorris, editor

Primarily published for Boy Scouts; contains features, how-to articles, comics, and reviews.

Braille Institute
741 North Vermont Avenue
Los Angeles, CA 90029
Russell Kirby, executive director

Offers educational programs for visually impaired children.

Braille Institute Press
741 North Vermont Avenue
Los Angeles, CA 90029
Jody Avery, children's editor

Publishes an anthology of children's literature in braille.

Brigham Young University Press
206 University Press Building
Provo, UT 84602
R. Kent Horsley, sales manager

Publishes books for teenagers and adults.

Brilliant Star
National Spiritual Assembly of the Baha'is of the US
915 Washington St., 3W
Evanston, IL 60202
Candice Hill, editor

Magazine with features for and by children, also poetry, games, puzzles, and stories.

Brooklyn Children's Museum
145 Brooklyn Avenue
Brooklyn, NY 11213
Mindy Duitz, director

B & R Samizdat Express
Box 161
West Roxbury, MA 02132
Richard Seltzer, publisher

Publishes fiction for children.

Brunner/Mazel
19 Union Square W.
New York, NY 10003
Ann Alhadef, children's editor

Publisher with a special interest in child abuse and family therapy.

Ça Va
Scholastic Inc.
730 Broadway
New York, NY 10003
Jacqueline Hall, editor

Magazine for second-year students of French.

California Weekly Explorer
285 E. Main St., #3
Tustin, CA 92680
Don Oliver, editor

Magazine on California history and geography written for and by children.

Calli's Tales
Box 1224
Palmetto, FL 33561
Annice E. Hunt, editor

Magazine about animals and their needs for survival with articles for and by young people.

Cambridge Book Company
Division of Simon & Schuster
888 Seventh Avenue
New York, NY 10106
Bill Moore, president

Publishes textbooks and specializes in English as a Second Language for any national origin.

Capital Children's Museum
800 Third Street, NE
Washington, DC 20002

Ann W. Lewin, director/curator

Hands-on museum for kids

Captain America
New World Entertainment/
    Marvel
387 Park Avenue South
New York, NY 10016
Stan Lee, publisher

Super-hero comic book

Care Bears
New World Entertainment/
    Marvel
387 Park Avenue South
New York, NY 10016
Stan Lee, publisher

Comic book

Career World
General Learning Corporation
3500 Western Avenue
Highland Park, IL 60035
Bonnie Bekken, editor

Helps young people explore possible career choices through books, pamphlets, and audio-visual materials.

Caspar Digest
Harvey Comics Entertainment
    Inc.
100 Wilshire Boulevard, Suite
    500
Santa Monica, CA 90401
Jeffrey Montgomery, publisher

Friendly ghost comic book

Chesapeake Planetarium
300 Cedar Road
Chesapeake, VA 23320

Robert J. Hitt, Jr., director/curator

Planetarium geared toward children

Chez Nous
Scholastic Inc.
730 Broadway
New York, NY 10003
Jacqueline Hall, editor

Magazine for third-year and advanced students of French

Child Life
Children's Better Health Institute
1100 Waterway Boulevard, Box
    567
Indianapolis, IN 46206
Steve Charles, editor

Entertaining magazine for and by children on good health habits

Children's Center Publications of California, Inc.
Box 885
Bonita, CA 92002
Peter Martin, children's editor

Publishes books on a variety of subjects for pre-school through the sixth grade.

Children's Digest
Benjamin Franklin Literary and
    Medical Society
1100 Waterway Boulevard
Indianapolis, IN 46206
Elizabeth A. Rinck, editor

Publishes stories, articles, puzzles, and activities with a health, nutrition, or safety theme.

Children's Learning Center
4660 East 62nd Street
Indianapolis, IN 46220
Nina Howard, publisher
Publishes books on reading readiness.

Children's Museum—Boston Museum Wharf
300 Congress Street
Boston, MA 02210
Kenneth Brecher, director/curator

Children's Museum—Detroit Public Schools
67 East Kirby
Detroit, MI 48202
Beatrice Parsons, director/curator

Children's Museum—Portland
3037 SW Second
Portland, OR 97212
Robert Bridgefored, director/curator

Children's Museum at La Habra
301 South Euclid
La Habra, CA 90631
Catherine Michaels, director/curator

Children's Museum of Denver
2121 Crescent Drive
Denver, CO 80211
Alby Segal, director/curator

Children's Museum of History, Natural History and Science
311 Main Street
Utica, NY 13501
Frank Viola, director/curator

The Children's Museum, Inc.— In Dartmouth
276 Gulf Road
South Dartmouth, MA 02748
Edith DeMello, director/curator

Children's Museum of Indianapolis
3000 North Meridien
Indianapolis, IN 46206
Peter Sterling, director/curator

Children's Museum of Maine
746 Stevens Avenue
Portland, ME 04103
Anthony W. Mollica, director/curator

Children's Museum of Manhattan
314 West 54th Street
New York, NY 10019
Bette Korman, director/curator

Children's Museum of Omaha
511 South 18th Street
Omaha, NE 68102
JoAnn Kimball, director/curator

Children's Museum of Rhode Island
58 Walcott Street
Pawtucket, RI 02860
Janice O'Donnell, director/curator
Exhibits include an early 20th-century marionette collection.

Children's Museum of Tampa, Inc.
9309 Floriland Mall
Tampa, FL 33612
Marian Winters, director/curator

Children's Playmate
Children's Better Health Institute
1100 Waterway Boulevard, Box 567
Indianapolis, IN 46206
Beth W. Thomas, executive director

Magazine focuses on health and entertainment.

Children's Press
Division of Regensteiner Publishing Enterprises
5440 North Cumberland
Chicago, IL 60656
John Winter, president

Publishes materials for the reading disabled.

Childs Play
Box 1333
Sterling Heights, MI 48311–1333
Phyllis Childs, president

Publishes books for the mentally disabled and developmentally delayed.

Child's World Books
980 North McLean Boulevard, Box 989
Elgin, IL 60121
Sandy Ziegler, children's editor

Publishes books on a wide variety of subjects for pre-school through fifth grade.

China Books & Periodicals
2929 24th Street
San Francisco, CA 94110
Foster Stockwell, children's editor

Publishes children's and adult books. Has a special interest in Chinese language and culture.

Christian Science Publishing Society
General Publications Department
One Norway Street
Boston, MA 02115
Thomas H. Fuller, Jr., manager of General Publications

Publishes books for children on family life, music, and religion.

Cinemagic
Starlog Press, Inc.
475 Park Avenue South
New York, NY 10016
David Hutchison, editor

Magazine teaches the fundamentals of fantasy film production to young people, covering all phases, from camera and lighting, to sets, costumes, and makeup.

Clarus Music, Ltd.
340 Bellevue Avenue
Yonkers, NY 10703
Selma Fass, president

Publishes music folios and plays for children.

Classical Calliope, The Muses' Magazine for Youth
Cobblestone Publishing, Inc.
20 Grove Street
Peterborough, NH 03458
Charles Baker III, editor

Introduces children to ancient history, literature, and culture.

Clavier's Piano Explorer
The Accent Publishing Company
200 Northfield Road
Northfield, IL 60093
Vickie S. Wills, Lorene Norton, editors

Magazine designed to supplement piano lessons, with features for and by children.

Cliffs Notes
Box 80728
Lincoln, NE 68501
J. Richard Spellman, president

Publishes teaching materials and review aids on literature.

Clubhouse
Your Story Hour
Box 15
Berrien Springs, MI 49103
Elaine Meseraull, editor

This magazine accompanies the "Your Story Hour" radio program.

Cobb County Youth Museum
649 Cheatham Hill Drive
Marietta, GA 30064
Anita S. Barton, director/curator

Cobblestone: The History Magazine for Young People
Cobblestone Publishing, Inc.
20 Grove Street
Peterborough, NH 03458
Beth Winston, editor

Each issue of this magazine focuses on a specific topic in American history.

Colgin Publishing
7657 Farmington Road
Manlius, NY 13104
Mary Louise N. Colgin, children's editor

Publishes language arts books for pre-school through sixth grade.

College Board
Publications Division
45 Columbus Avenue
New York, NY 10023
Carolyn Trager, children's editor

Publishes books, software, films, etc. for career development and language arts.

Colonial Williamsburg
The Colonial Williamsburg Foundation, Department of Publications
Williamsburg, VA 23185
Joseph N. Rountree, director of publications

Publishes books for children and adults on US Colonial history, crafts, and how-to-books.

Columbia Scholastic Press Association
Box 11, Central Mall Rx, Columbia University
New York, NY 10017
Edmund J. Sullivan, executive director

Want to start a school newspaper? This group will help.

Comic Magazine Association of America
60 East 42nd Street
New York, NY 10017
J. Dudley Waldner, CAE, executive director
Association of publishers, engravers, and printers of comic books.

Comics Buyers Guide
Krause Publications
700 East State Street
Iola, WI 54990
John Koenig, publisher
Publication for comic book fans and collectors. Contains the most recent news about comics and the people who write and draw them.

Communication Skill Builders, Inc.
3130 North Dodge Boulevard, Box 42050
Tucson, AZ 85733
Patti Hartmann, managing editor
Publishes picture books, auditory and visual dictionaries, language arts books, and mathematics materials.

Community Council for the Arts Children's Museum
111 East Caswell Street
Kinston, NC 28501
Mark E. Brown, director/curator

Compcare Publications
2415 Annapolis Lane
Minneapolis, MN 55441
Jane Noland, children's editor
Publishes books on family life, health, alcoholism, drug abuse, eating disorders, child abuse, and parenting.

Computer Science Press, Inc.
1803 Research Boulevard
Rockville, MD 20850
Barbara B. Friedman, president
Publishes books on computer software, mathematics, and the sciences for children.

Conan the Barbarian
New World Entertainment/
    Marvel
387 Park Avenue South
New York, NY 10016
Stan Lee, publisher
Comic book

Consumers Union
256 Washington Street
Mt. Vernon, NY 10550
Rhoda H. Karpatkin, executive director
Specializes in books on consumer education, health, and economics for children and adults.

Cora Hartshorn Arboretum
324 Forest Drive South
Short Hills, NJ 07078
Elizabeth Naughton, director/curator

Council for Exceptional Children
1920 Association Drive
Reston, VA 22091–1589
Jeptha V. Greer, executive director

Works with and publishes material for the reading disabled, mentally disabled, behaviorally disabled, and gifted child.

Council on Interracial Books for Children Inc.
1841 Broadway
New York, NY 10023
Harriet Brown, president

Publishes books on a wide variety of topics.

Coyote Point Museum for Environmental Protection
Coyote Point Park
San Mateo, CA 94404
Linda Liebes, director/curator

Features games, computer games, films, exhibits, and graphics depicting six ecological zones found in the San Francisco Bay area.

Cracked
Globe Communications
535 Fifth Avenue
New York, NY 10017
Robert C. Sproul, publisher

Satirical magazine

Crane Publishing Company Division of MLP
1301 Hamilton Avenue
Trenton, NJ 08629
Barbara J. Crane, president

Specializes in books for Spanish-speaking or other bilingual students.

Creative Kids
GCT, Inc.
Box 6448
Mobile, AL 36660
Fay L. Gold, editor

This magazine publishes work by children.

Creative Storytime Press
Box 572
Minneapolis, MN 55440
D. Owidfield, president and
    editor-in-chief

Publishes instructional aids for young children and specializes in storytelling.

Crestwood House
Box 3427, Highway 665
Mankato, MN 56001
Darel Jacobsen, children's editor

Books and educational materials for K-9, specializing in the reading disabled.

Cricket Magazine
Carus Corporation
Box 300
Peru, IL 61354
Marianne Carus, editor-in-chief

Literature for and by children

Crown Publishers
Children's Book Department
225 Park Avenue South
New York, NY 10003
Simon Boughton, president

Publishes a wide variety of books for children.

Current Events
Field Publications
245 Long Hill Road
Middletown, CT 06457
Terry Borton, editor
Features on national and world events for and by children

Current Health 1: A Beginning Guide to Health Education
General Learning Corporation
3500 West Avenue
Highland Park, IL 60035
Laura Ruekberg, executive editor
Health magazines geared to grades 4–7

Current Science
Field Publications
245 Long Hill Road
Middletown, CT 06457
Vincent Marteka, senior editor
Publishes reports on the latest scientific advances and teaches science basics. Some articles by children.

Das Rad
Scholastic Inc.
730 Broadway
New York, NY 10003
Jacqueline Hall, editor
Publication for first-year students of German

Dawn Publications
14618 Tyler Foote Road
Nevada City, CA 95959

Richard McCord, children's editor
Publishes children's books on the environment, animals, and family life.

Denoyer-Geppert Science Company
5215 North Ravenswood Avenue
Chicago, IL 60640
Richard Gilbert, president
Specializes in science and health books for children of all ages.

Der Roller
Scholastic Inc.
730 Broadway
New York, NY 10003
Irene Marner, editor
Publication for third-year and advanced students of German

Detective Comics
DC Comics, Inc.
355 Lexington Avenue
New York, NY 10017
Julius Schwartz, editor
Comic book

Dial Books for Young Readers
Subsidiary of E. P. Dutton
375 Hudson Street
New York, NY 10014
Janet Chenery, Paula Wiseman,
    Toby Sherry, children's editors
Publishes books for pre-school through twelfth grade.

Dirt
230 Park Avenue
New York, NY 10169
Mary Kaye Schilling, executive editor
Quarterly magazine for teenage boys, focusing on music, health, relationships, trends, and sports.

Discoveries
Beacon Hill Press
2923 Troost Avenue
Kansas City, MO 64109
Molly Mitchell, editor
Magazine which supplements Sunday school lessons

Discovery Museum
51 Park Street
Essex Junction, VT 05452
Kris Crouchley, director/curator

Discovery Place and Nature Museum
Science Museums of Charlotte, Inc.
301 North Tryon Street
Charlotte, NC 28202
Freda H. Nicholson, director/curator
This museum uses "open storage" to allow visitors to see collections of minerals, shells, insects, and butterflies. Visitors can also view specimen preparation.

Displays for Schools, Inc.
Box 163
Gainesville, FL 32602–0163
Herbert C. DuPree, president
Specializes in multimedia kits, workbooks, and paperbacks.

DOK Publishers
Box 605
East Aurora, NY 14052
James A. West, children's editor
Specializes in publishing books for the gifted and talented child.

Dolphin Log
The Cousteau Society
8440 Santa Monica Boulevard
Los Angeles, CA 90069
Beth Kneeland, editor
The purpose of this magazine is to "delight, instruct and instill an environmental ethic and understanding of the interconnectedness of all living organisms."

Doubleday & Company
Books for Young Readers
245 Park Avenue
New York, NY 10017
Diane Arico, children's editor
Publishes dictionaries, encyclopedias, fiction, and picture books.

Down Beat Magazine
180 West Park Avenue
Elmhurst, IL 60126
John Ephland, editor
Youth-oriented music magazine

Drama Book Publishers
Box 816, Gracie Station
New York, NY 10028
Ralph Pine, marketing director

*Publishers of books on drama,
theater, and music.*

Dramatic Publishing Company
311 Washington Street
Woodstock, IL 60098
Christopher Sergel, owner

*Publishes books on drama and
plays.*

Dramatists Play Service
440 Park Avenue South
New York, NY 10016
F. Andrew Leslie, president

*One of the two largest script
publishers in the US.*

Dream Guys Magazine
P.O. Box 7042
New York, NY 10128
Grace Catalano, editor

*Magazine geared to teenage
girls*

Duckburg Times
3010 Wilshire Boulevard, Suite
362
Los Angeles, CA 90010
Dana Gabbard, editor

Disney comics

Durst Publications
29–28 41st Avenue
Long Island City, NY 11101
Sanford J. Durst, president

*Publishes children's books on
art and hobbies (particularly nu-
mismatics and philatelics) and
children's classics.*

**E. P. Press (Eleanora Patterson
Press)**
Box 343
Putney, VT 05346
Eleanora Patterson, president

*Publishes books on family life
and sex education.*

Early Educators Press
Box 1177
Lake Alfred, FL 33850
Barbara Johnson, president

*Publishing house that special-
izes in cookbooks for K–4.*

Earth Science
American Geological Institute
4220 King Street
Alexandria, VA 22302
Kathy Petrini, editor

*Magazine for students interested
in the Earth Sciences*

Educational Solutions
95 University Place
New York, NY 10003
Dr. Gattegno, children's editor

*Publishes books on foreign lan-
guages, language arts,
mathematics, pyschology, philosophy, and literacy.*

Educators Progress Service
214 Center Street
Randolph, WI 53956
Kathy Nehmer, marketing director

Publishes guides to free materials.

El Sol
Scholastic Inc.
730 Broadway
New York, NY 10003
Christine Haylett, editor

Magazine for second-year students of Spanish.

Electronic Gaming Monthly
Sendai Publishing Group, Inc.
1920 Highland Avenue
Lombard, IL 60148
Steve Harris, publisher/editor-in-chief

Buyer's guide for electronic games

Enchanted World Doll Museum
615 North Main
Mitchell, SD 57301
Eunice T. Reese, director/curator

Encyclopaedia Britannica Educational Corporation
425 North Michigan Avenue
Chicago, IL 60611
Ralph C. Wagner, president

Publishers of the Encyclopaedia Britannica, Great Books, and many other publications.

Enfantaisie: La Revue des Enfants
2603 SE 32nd Avenue
Portland, OR 97202
Viviane Gould, editor

Magazine for children, grades 3–10, studying French.

EPM Publications, Inc.
1003 Turkey Run Road
McLean, VA 22101
Evelyn P. Metzger, president

Publishes books on crafts, needlework, quilting, home economics, with a special interest in Native Americans.

Eugene Field House & Toy Museum
634 South Broadway
St. Louis, MO 63102
John Scholz, director/curator

Ewoks
New World Entertainment/
   Marvel
387 Park Avenue South
New York, NY 10016
Stan Lee, publisher

Comic book based on Star Wars' *furry heroes.*

Exploratorium
3601 Lyon Street
San Francisco, CA 94123
Goery Delacote, director

Museum for kids

The Eye Magazine
The Resource Center, YMCA of
   Delaware

11th and Washington Streets
Wilmington, DE 19801
Doris Bolt, publisher
Magazine featuring articles on children and the media, written by children.

Faces: The Magazine About People
Cobblestone Publishing
20 Grove Street
Peterborough, NH 03458
Carolyn P. Yoder, editor
Anthropological magazine published in cooperation with the American Museum of Natural History.

Fan Club Directory
2730 Baltimore Avenue
Pueblo, CO 81003
Directory of fan clubs for a variety of entertainers, actors, and sports personalities.

Flash
DC Comics, Inc.
355 Lexington Avenue
New York, NY 10017
Julius Schwartz, editor
Super-hero comic book

Flash Gordon
King Features Syndicate
235 East 45th Street
New York, NY 10017
William Harris, editor
Futuristic comic book

Freebies
P.O. Box 20283

Santa Barbara, CA 93120
Abel Magana, editor
Magazine that lists free and low-cost items

Friend
The Church of Jesus Christ of
   Latter-Day Saints
50 East North Temple
Salt Lake City, UT 84150
Vivian Paulsen, editor
Magazine that publishes features for children, based on the principles of the Church of Jesus Christ of Latter-Day Saints.

Georgia Southern College Museum
Rosenwald Building
Georgia Southern College
Statesboro, GA 30458
Delma Presley, director/curator
Museum with specific exhibits geared for kids.

GI Joe Magazine
Lorimar Publishing Group
300 Madison Avenue
New York, NY 10017
Jim Buckley, editor
Sports and adventure magazine for boys.

Glamour Magazine
360 Madison Avenue
New York, NY 10017
Ruth Whitney, editor
Beauty and fashion magazine

Golden Press
Western Publishing Company Inc.
850 Third Avenue
New York, NY 10022
Doris Duenewald, publisher
Publishers of the Golden Books series

Grindstone Bluff Museum
Box 7965
Shreveport, LA 71507
J. Ashley Sibley, Jr., director/ curator
Archaeological museum with programs for gifted students.

Hannah Lindahl Children's Museum
1402 South Main Street
Mishawaka, IN 46544
Betty Hans, director/curator
This museum exhibits historical objects from local homes and factories, plus Japanese artifacts from Mishawaka's sister city.

Happy Times
Concordia Publishing House
3558 South Jefferson Avenue
St. Louis, MO 63118
Earl Gaulke, editor
Christian magazine for children, featuring stories, games, prayers, poems, and puzzles.

Harper Junior Books
10 East 53rd Street
New York, NY 10022
Joanna Cotler, publisher

Publishes a variety of books for kids and teenagers.

The Health Adventure
501 Biltmore Avenue
Asheville, NC 28801
Connie McConnell, director/ curator
Exhibits contain oversize models which dramatize body systems and functions.

Highlights for Children
2300 West Fifth Avenue
Box 269
Columbus, OH 43215
Kent L. Brown, Jr., editor
Popular doctor's waiting-room magazine. Contains fiction, non-fiction, crafts, verse, readers' contributions, and "thinking activities."

Hoy Día
Scholastic Inc.
730 Broadway
New York, NY 10003
Jacqueline Hall, editor
Magazine for third-year and advanced students of Spanish.

Humpty Dumpty's Magazine
Benjamin Franklin Literary and Medical Society
1100 Waterway Boulevard
Indianapolis, IN 46206
Christine French Clark, editor
Magazine which contains articles, stories, puzzles, and activities stressing health, nutrition, and exercise.

Information Center on Children's Cultures
331 East 38th Street
New York, NY 10016
Melinda Greenblatt, chief librarian

International resource for children who want information on children of other nations, e.g. clothing, art.

Inka Dinka Ink Children's Press
4741 Guerley Road
Cincinnati, OH 45238
Patricia Bowling, president

Publishes books for elementary-school age children.

Institute for the Advancement of Philosophy for Children
Montclair State College
Upper Montclair, NJ 07043
Matthew Lipman, director

Publishes books on educational theory and philosophy for children.

International Concerns Committee for Children
911 Cypress Drive
Boulder, CO 80303
AnnaMarie Merrill, treasurer

Works with adoptions for children from foreign countries.

International Gymnast
Sundbysports, Inc.
225 Brooks, Box G
Oceanside, CA 92054
Dwight Normile, editor

Publishes information on international gymnastic events and personalities.

Jack & Jill
Children's Health Publications
1100 Waterway Boulevard, Box 567
Indianapolis, IN 46206
Steve Charles, editor

Features articles written for and by children.

Jacksonville Museum of Arts and Sciences
1025 Gulf Life Drive
Jacksonville, FL 32207
William J. Martin, director/curator

Museum with extensive exhibits geared to kids.

Josephine D. Randall Junior Museum
199 Museum Way
San Francisco, CA 94114
Dr. A. K. Conragan, director/curator

Junior Scholastic
Scholastic Inc.
730 Broadway
New York, NY 10003
Lee Baier, editor

Social studies magazine written for and by children.

Karshner Memorial Museum
309 Fourth Street, NE
Puyallup, WA 98371
Brooke Thompson, director/curator

Museum which exhibits fossils, minerals, and sealife of the Northwest coast. Has special hours for the Puyallup School District.

Keeping Posted with NCSY
National Conference of Synagogue Youth
45 West 36th Street
New York, NY 10018
Rabbi Krupka, editor

Features articles for and by Jewish children and teenagers.

Kid City
Children's Television Workshop
One Lincoln Plaza
New York, NY 10023
Maureen Hunter-Bone, editor

Magazine to develop children's reading skills. Contains games, puzzles, comics, activities, posters, articles, etc.

Kidspace Museum
390 South El Molino Avenue
Pasadena, CA 91101
Elaine Fleming, director/curator

Know Your World Extra!
Field Publications
245 Long Hill Road
Middletown, CT 06457
Terry Borton, editor

Current events magazine geared to problem readers. Some articles written by kids.

Laura Ingalls Wilder Home and Museum
Rocky Ridge Farm
Mansfield, MO 65704
Irene Lichty, director/curator

Place where the author of the "Little House" books lived.

Laura Ingalls Wilder Museum and Tourist Center
Walnut Grove, MN 56180
Shirley Knakmuhs, director/curator

Museum located in the small town that the "Little House" books (and subsequent television series) made famous.

Listen
6830 Laurel Street, NW
Washington, DC 20012

Magazine written for and by young people on alcohol, drug, and tobacco dependency.

Lori Brock Children's Museum
3803 Chester Avenue
Bakersfield, CA 93301
Barbara Jewett, director/curator

Los Angeles Children's Museum
310 North Main Street
Los Angeles, CA 90012
Jack Armstrong, director/curator

Louisville Art Gallery
301 York Street
Louisville, KY 40203
Roberta L. Williams, director/curator

Art gallery with exhibits geared to children and children's art.

Lutz Children's Museum
247 South Main Street
Manchester, CT 06040
Steven Ling, director/curator

Mad Magazine
485 Madison Avenue
New York, NY 10022
Albert B. Feldstein, editor

Cartoon magazine

Mademoiselle Magazine
350 Madison Avenue
New York, NY 10017
Amy Levin Cooper, editor

Beauty and fashion magazine

Mandrake the Magician
King Features Syndicate
235 East 45th Street
New York, NY 10017
Lee Falk, creator

Adventure and fantasy comic book

Mark Twain Boyhood Home/ Museum
208 Hill Street
Hannibal, MO 63401
Henry Sweets, director/curator

Exhibits consist mainly of restored rooms and Mark Twain memorabilia.

Marvel Comics
387 Park Avenue South
New York, NY 10016
Tom DeFalco, editor

Comic book publisher

Mary Merritt Doll Museum
Route 2
Douglassville, PA 19518
Mary Merritt, director/curator

McCurdy Historical Doll Museum
246 North 100 East
Provo, UT 84601
Shirley B. Paxman, director/ curator

Merlyn's Pen
Box 1058
East Greenwich, RI 02818
R. James Stahl, editor

Magazine that publishes kids' writing and artwork.

Muncie Children's Museum
306 South Walnut
Muncie, IN 47305
Beth E. Davis, director/curator

My Friend: A Magazine for Boys & Girls
Daughters of St. Paul
50 St. Paul's Avenue
Jamaica Plain, MA 02130
Anne Joan, editor

Magazine written for and by children.

My Weekly Reader
Field Publications
245 Long Hill Road
Middletown, CT 06457
Terry Borton, editor-in-chief

Prints high-interest readings on current events.

National Future Farmer
Future Farmers of America
Box 15130
Alexandria, VA 22309
Wilson W. Carnes, editor
*Articles of interest to young
people planning a career in agri-
culture.*

National Geographic World
National Geographic Society
17th and M Streets, NW
Washington, DC 20036
Pat Robbins, editor
*Features and news written for
and by children. Numerous
photographs.*

**National Health Information
Clearinghouse**
US Department of Health and
Human Services
P.O. Box 1133
Washington, DC 20013
Louis W. Sullivan, secretary of
Health and Human Services
*General information and pam-
phlets available on all health-
related topics.*

**National School Orchestra As-
sociation**
345 Maxwell Drive
Pittsburgh, PA 15236
Norman Mellin, executive director
*Sponsors a contest for original
musical compositions created
by school groups, with a
$1,000 prize.*

**Netherland Inn Boat Yard Com-
plex**
**Jeremy Honeycutt Log Cabin
Children's Museum**
2144 Netherland Inn Road
Kingsport, TN 37660
Muriel C. Spoden, director/
curator
Frontier American settlement

New Britain Youth Museum
30 High Street
New Britain, CT 06051
Alan J. Krauss, director/curator

New Kids on the Block
Harvey Comics Entertainment,
Inc.
100 Wilshire Boulevard, Suite
500
Santa Monica, CA 90401
Jeffrey Montgomery, publisher
*Comic book based on the pop
group*

Nights
Viz Communications Inc.
440 Brannan Street
San Francisco, CA 94107
Seiji Horibuchi, publisher
*Science-fiction adventure comic
book.*

Odyssey
Kalmbach Publishing Company
1027 North Seventh Street
Milwaukee, WI 53233
Nancy Mack, editor
*Magazine that prints articles for
and by children on astronomy
and space science.*

Olomeinu-Our World
Torah Umesorah, National Society for Hebrew Day Schools
5723 18th Avenue
Brooklyn, New York 11204
Rabbi Yaakiv Fruchter, Rabbi Nosson Scherman, editors
Magazine for young Jewish students

On the Line
Mennonite Publishing House
616 Walnut Avenue
Scottdale, PA 15683
Ellen Parlar, editor
Publishes articles on nature and media. Primary focus is on God and Christianity in the natural world.

Orchard House
Louisa May Alcott Memorial Association
Box 343
Concord, MA 01742
Jayne Gordon, executive director
House where Louisa May Alcott wrote Little Women. *The association sponsors lectures and tours for children.*

Our Little Friend
Pacific Press Publishing Association
Box 7000
Boise, ID 83707
Aileen Andres Sox, editor
Children's magazine from the Seventh Day Adventist Church.

Perelman Antique Toy Museum
270 South Second Street
Philadelphia, PA 19106–3905
Leon J. Perelman, director/curator

Plays, the Drama Magazine for Young People
120 Boylston Street
Boston, MA 02116
Sylvia K. Burack, editor
Magazine that provides schools and clubs with new, royalty-free plays and programs.

Please Touch Museum
210 North 21st Street
Philadelphia, PA 19103
Portia Hamilton Sperr, director/curator
"Hands-on" museum for children.

Pockets
The Upper Room
1908 Grand
Nashville, TN 37202
Janet McNish Bugge, editor
Magazine with features by and for children "to help children lay a foundation for a vital spiritual life through prayer and an awareness of God."

Portsmouth Children's Museum
Court Street
Portsmouth, VA 23705
Dr. Nancy J. Melton, director
Trish Pfeifer, curator

The Putnam and Grosset Group
200 Madison Avenue
New York, NY 10016
Margaret Frith, president

Publishes a wide variety of books for kids from pre-school through high school.

Que Tal
Scholastic Inc.
730 Broadway
New York, NY 10003
Christine Kenner, editor

Magazine for first-year students of Spanish.

Quinto Lingo
American National Heritage Association
Box 9340
Alexandria, VA 22304
Endel Peedo, editor

Educational and cultural magazine in 7 languages oriented to American ethnic populations and language students.

Ranger Rick
The National Wildlife Federation
1412 16th Street, NW
Washington, DC 20036
Gerald Bishop, editor

Magazine for kids on how to properly use, respect, and enjoy natural resources.

Read
Field Publications
245 Long Hill Road
Middletown, CT 06457
Terry Borton, editor

Magazine that publishes articles written for and by kids to help build reading skills and vocabulary.

Rensselaer County Junior Museum
282 Fifth Avenue
Troy, NY 12182
Ralph Pascale, director/curator

Right On!
Sterling's Magazines, Inc.
355 Lexington Avenue
New York, NY 10017
Cynthia M. Horner, executive editor

Fan magazine

Sassy
230 Park Avenue
New York, NY 10169
Jane Pratt, editor in chief

Magazine for teenage girls, focusing on fashion, beauty, health, music, and trends.

Scholastic Action
Scholastic Inc.
730 Broadway
New York, NY 10003
Jeri Shapiro, editor

Magazine published for "slow" readers.

Scholastic Math
Scholastic Inc.
730 Broadway
New York, NY 10003
Sue Macy, editor

Publishes reviews of computer software, math puzzles and games, learning ideas, and trends in math.

Scholastic News
Scholastic Inc.
730 Broadway
New York, NY 10003
Kathy Johnson, editor

Magazine about people, places, and news for elementary school children.

Scholastic Scope
Scholastic Inc.
730 Broadway
New York, NY 10003
Fran Claro, editor

Features for and by children to encourage slower readers.

Scholastic Sprint
Scholastic Inc.
730 Broadway
New York, NY 10003
Jeri Shapiro, editor

Magazine for children in grades 4–6.

Science Museum of Greater Hartford
950 Trout Brook Drive
West Hartford, CT 06119
Robert Content, director/curator

Scienceland
Scienceland Inc.
501 Fifth Avenue
New York, NY 10017
A. H. Matano, editor

Science magazine which promotes reading and early science education for young children.

Seedling Series: Short Story International
International Cultural Exchange
6 Sheffield Road
Great Neck, NY 11021
Sylvia Tankel, editor

International short stories for young readers.

Sesame Street Magazine
Children's Television Workshop
1 Lincoln Plaza
New York, NY 10023
Marge Kennedy, editor in chief

Companion magazine to Sesame Street television show.

Seventeen
Triangle Communications
850 Third Avenue
New York, NY 10022
Midge Richardson, editor-in-chief

Magazine for teenage girls focusing on fashion, beauty, health, food, and decorating.

Shofar
Senior Publications Ltd.
339 N. Main St.
New City, NY 10956
Gerald Grayson, editor

Magazine written for and by children, with articles focusing on Jewish heritage.

16 Magazine
Katherine Young, 16 Magazine Inc.
157 West 57th Street
New York, NY 10019
Randi Reisfeld, editor

A youth-oriented entertainment magazine

Sports Illustrated for Kids
Time & Life Building, Rockefeller Center
New York, NY 10020
Craig Neff, managing editor

Version of Sports Illustrated for and about young athletes.

Stone Soup, the Magazine by Children
Children's Art Foundation
Box 83
Santa Cruz, CA 95063
Gerry Mandel, William Rubel, editors

Publishes articles and artwork by children.

Story Friends
Mennonite Publishing House
616 Walnut Avenue
Scottdale, PA 15683
Marjorie Waybill, editor

Children's drawings, puzzles, activities, and feature articles, created by children.

Sunrise Children's Museum and Planetarium
746 Myrtle Road
Charleston, WV 25314
Frankie McCain, director/curator

Super Teen
Sterling's Magazines
355 Lexington Avenue
New York, NY 10017
Sharon Gintzler, editor

Fan magazine

Superman
DC Comics, Inc.
355 Lexington Avenue
New York, NY 10017
Julius Schwartz, publisher

Super-hero comic book

Surprises, Activities for Kids and Parents
Children's Surprises Inc.
Box 236
Chanhassen, MN 55317
Jeanne Palmer, Peggy Simenson, editors

Fun stuff for kids pre-school through sixth grade.

Swimming World & Junior Swimmer
Swimming World Publications
Box 45497
Los Angeles, CA 90045
Bob Ingram, editor

Magazines for swimmers of all ages.

Tapori
New Inc./Fourth World Movement
7600 Willow Hill Dr.
Landover, MD 20785
Fanchette Clement-Fanelli, editor

Publishes articles for and by children to help children from all backgrounds learn from each other.

Teen
Petersen Publishing Company
8490 Sunset Boulevard
Los Angeles, CA 90069
Robert F. MacLeod, editorial director and executive publisher
Fashion and beauty magazine for teenage girls.

Teen Beat Magazine
215 Lexington Avenue
New York, NY 10016
Karen L. Williams, editor
Youth-oriented magazine

Teen Machine
Sterling's Magazines
355 Lexington Avenue
New York, NY 10017
Marie Therese Morreale, editor
Fan magazine

Teenage Mutant Ninja Turtles
Mirage Studios
26 Center Street
Northhampton, MA 01060
Peter Laird, publisher
Comic book starring the superhero turtles.

Teens Today
Nazarene Publishing House
6401 The Pasco
Kansas City, MO 64131
Karen DeSollar, editor

Religious magazine for teenagers.

3-2-1 Contact Magazine
Children's Television Workshop
1 Lincoln Plaza
New York, NY 10023
Jonathan Rosenbloom, editor in chief
Companion magazine for 3-2-1 Contact Television Show

Tiger Beat Magazine
1086 Teaneck Road
Teaneck, NJ 07666
Mary J. Edrei, editor
Youth-oriented music magazine

Toy Train Museum
Paradise Lane
Strasburg, PA 17579
Betty Perini, director/curator

Tutti Frutti
Jimmijack Publishing Company, Inc.
807 Vivian Court
Baldwin, NY 11510
Jack Borgen, publisher
Fan magazine

U*S* Kids
Field Publications
245 Long Hill Road
Middletown, CT 06457
Terry Borton, editor
News magazine that strives to connect kids to the world around them.

Victorian Doll Museum
4332 Buffalo Road
North Chili, NY 14514
Linda Greenfield, director/curator

Wee Wisdom
Unity School of Christianity
Unity Village, MO 64065
Verle Bell, editor

Religious magazine for young children.

Writing!
General Learning Corporation
60 Revere Drive
Northbrook, IL 60062
Alan Lenhoff, editor

Magazine to encourage junior and senior high school students to write and write well.

YABA World
Young American Bowling Alliance
5301 South 76th Street
Greendale, WI 53129
Peggy Larson, editor

Magazine for young bowlers.

Young Audiences
115 East 92nd Street
New York, NY 10128
Warren H. Yost, executive director

Sends professional performing artists to elementary and secondary school for special programs.

Young People Today
Gemstones Adventures, Inc.
Box 19438
Los Angeles, CA 90019–9990
Camille C. Steverson, editor

Communications, business, and publishing magazine for kids.

Zillions
(formerly Penny Power)
101 Truman Avenue
Yonkers, NY 10703–1057
Charlotte Boucher, editor

Consumer information magazine for young people. Runs tests and surveys with kids on products and services. Kids review movies, television, and music.

NEED A HELPING HAND OR A SYMPATHETIC EAR?

Included in this category are a lot of organizations that can help you, your family, or your friends with a lot of problems. Hotline numbers have been included for some of the organizations.

Adoptees' Liberty Movement Association
P.O. Box 154
Washington Bridge Station
New York, NY 10033

Maintains a data bank and offers advice on searching for adoptive parents and children.

Aid to Adoption of Special Kids
3530 Grand Avenue
Oakland, CA 94610
Bob Diamond, executive director

Information and referrals for adopting older, handicapped, and other special kids.

Al-Anon Family Group Headquarters, Inc.
P.O. Box 862
Midtown Station
New York, NY 10018–0862
Myrna Hammersley, executive director

Organization which helps families of alcoholics.

Alateen
Al-Anon Family Group Headquarters, Incorporated
P.O. Box 862, Midtown Station
New York, NY 10018–0862
Bonnie Cummings, administrator

Alateen is a fellowship of young Al-Anon members whose lives have been affected by someone else's drinking.

Alexander Graham Bell Association for the Deaf
3417 Volta Place, NW
Washington, DC 20007
Lucy Cuzon Du Rest, director of publications

Publishes books and special materials for the deaf.

American Anorexia/Bulimia Association
133 Cedar Lane
Teaneck, NJ 07666
Caaron Belcher Willinger, executive director

Information, advice, and referrals for people with eating disorders.

American Association of Psychiatric Services for Children
1200–C Scottsdale Road, Suite 225
Rochester, NY 14624
Dr. Sydney Koret, executive director

Information and referrals

American Association of Suicidology
2459 South Ash
Denver, CO 80222
Julie Perlman, executive officer

Dedicated to research and the prevention of unnecessary deaths. Publications available.

American Cancer Society
159 Clifton Road
Atlanta, GA 30329
William M. Tipping, executive vice-president

Largest cancer counseling, referral, and research organization.

American Conference of Therapeutic Self-Help/Self-Health/Social Action Clubs
710 Lodi Street
Syracuse, NY 13203

Shirley Mae Burghard, RN, executive director

Provides information and materials on self-help groups nationwide.

American Foundation for the Blind
Publications Division
15 West 16th Street
New York, NY 10011
William Gallagher, executive director

Publishes books on blindness and visual impairment.

American Kidney Fund
6110 Executive Boulevard, Suite 1010
Rockville, MD 20852
Francis J. Soldovere, executive director

Provides support and information for all patients who have kidney disease or need dialysis or transplants.

American Society for Deaf Children
814 Thayer Avenue
Silver Spring, MD 20910
Millie Maisel, office manager

Information for deaf children on education and opportunities.

American Society for the Prevention of Cruelty to Animals
Education Department
441 East 92nd Street
New York, NY 10128

Michael E. Kaufmann, director of education

America's oldest humane society provides assistance and resources on humane education.

America's Pride Program/World Youth Against Drugs
National Parent's Resource Institute for Drug Education
50 Hurt Plaza, Suite 210
Atlanta, GA 30303
Lisa Ellsworth, national youth director

Dedicated to creating an international generation of drug-free youth.

Association for Blind Living and Education
4139 Regent Avenue, N
Minneapolis, MN 55422
Diane Zeigler, director

Organization for blind and visually impaired children and teens, primarily those living in Minnesota.

Association for Death Education and Counseling
638 Prospect Avenue
Hartford, CT 06105
M. Suzanne C. Berry, managing director

Publications, conferences, and information sharing.

Batterers Anonymous
1269 NE Street
San Bernardino, CA 92405

Jerry M. Goffman, PhD, founder

Offers help for families of battered spouses.

Bereavement Center
Westchester Jewish Community Services
172 South Broadway
White Plains, NY 10605
Eugene Aronowitz, executive director

Information, therapy/discussion group for children who have lost a family member.

The Bridge, Inc.
325 West 85th Street
New York, NY 10024
Murray Itzkowitz, executive director

Focuses on rehabilitation of the mentally ill.

Cancer Care, Inc.
1180 Avenue of the Americas
New York, NY 10036
Diane Blum, executive director

Education and counseling for cancer patients and their families.

Cancer Connection
4410 Main
Kansas City, MO 64111
Kathie Nicholson, executive director

Group that matches victims with those who have the same disease, for mutual support.

Candlelighters Childhood Cancer Foundation
1901 Pennsylvania Avenue, NW, Suite 1001
Washington, DC 20006
Grace Powers Monaco, board chairman
Groups of parents of children who have or have had cancer help one another, keep informed of research, and lobby to conquer cancer.

Cansurmount
c/o American Cancer Society
1599 Clifton Road
Atlanta, GA 30334
Dr. Morton Bard, executive officer
A division of the American Cancer Society, this group forms self-help liaisons between doctor and patient.

Center for Death Education and Research
University of Minnesota
Minneapolis, MN 55455
Robert L. Fulton, PhD, director
Information and publications available.

Center for Sickle Cell Diseases
2121 Georgia Avenue, NW
Washington, DC 20059
Roland B. Scott, MD, director
Information and referrals.

Center for Thanatology Research and Education
391 Atlantic Avenue
Brooklyn, NY 11217
Books, journals, bibliographies, and referrals to other organizations to help people cope with death.

Child Abuse Listening Medication, Inc.
P.O. Box 718
Santa Barbara, CA 93102
Cheryl Simmen, executive director
Works toward prevention of child abuse.

Child Find of America
P.O. Box 277
New Paltz, NY 12561
(800) 431-5005
Carolyn Zogg, associate director
Parents of missing children can make contact with their youngsters through this organization.

Child Welfare League of America
440 First Street, NW, Suite 310
Washington, DC 20001
David S. Liederman, executive director
Publishes materials regarding children in distress; any kind of distress.

Childhelp USA, Inc.
6463 Independence Avenue
Woodland Hills, CA 91370

Sara O'Meara, board chairman

Works to prevent child abuse. Also sponsors the Village of Childhelp, a residential program for abused children.

Children in Hospitals
31 Wilshire Park
Needham, MA 02192
Barbara K. Popper, founder

Information about the needs of children who are hospitalized.

Children of Ageing Parents
2761 Trenton Road
Levittown, PA 19056
Mirca Leberti, executive director

Self-help group designed to help children care for their parents, or grandchildren to help their grandparents.

Children of Deaf Adults
Box 30715
Santa Barbara, CA 93130
Millie Brother, founder

Society of hearing children of deaf parents who are interested in sharing experiences.

Children's Blood Foundation
424 East 62nd Street, Room 1045
New York, NY 10021
Corinne Curry, executive director

Help for children with rare blood conditions or chronic diseases affecting the blood.

Children's Defense Fund
122 C Street, NW
Washington, DC 20001
Marian Wright Edelman, president

Long-term advocates for children. That means they go to bat for kids.

Committee for Children
172 20th Avenue
Seattle, WA 98122
Karen Bacheider, executive director

Provides information and advocacy for children; especially interested in kidnapping by a parent who does not have legal custody.

Choice in Dying
250 West 57th Street
New York, NY 10107
James R. Sheffield, president

Promotion of euthanasia (mercy killing), the living will, and the right to die.

Concerned United Birthparents, Inc.
2000 Walker Street
Des Moines, IA 50317
Janet Fenton, president

Works toward opening birth records for adoptees and birth parents.

Daughters and Sons United
840 Guadalupe Parkway
San Jose, CA 95110
Dr. Henry Giarretto, executive director

Information exchange and support system for sexually abused children and their families.

Divorce Anonymous
P.O. Box 5313
Chicago, IL 60680
Melody Broadwell, president

Provides support for divorcees and their families.

Do It Now Foundation
P.O. Box 27568
Phoenix, AZ 85285
James Parker, executive director

Not a membership organization, this foundation publishes a variety of booklets, posters, and reports on drug and alcohol issues.

Drug-Anon Focus
Park West Station
P.O. Box 20806
New York, NY 10025

Offers help for drug abusers and their families.

Drugs Anonymous
P.O. Box 473
Ansonia Station
New York, NY 10023
Mary Lou Phippen, secretary

Focuses on abuse of prescription drugs, cocaine, and marijuana.

Emotions Anonymous
P.O. Box 4245
St. Paul, MN 55104
William Roath, coordinator

Sets up local discussion groups to promote emotional health in a self-help atmosphere.

Families Anonymous
P.O. Box 528
Van Nuys, CA 91408
(800) 736-9805

Help for drug-abusing teens and their families.

Family Service America
11700 West Lake Park Drive
Milwaukee, WI 53224
Geneva B. Johnson, CEO/president

Organization geared toward helping families under stress.

Foundation of Thanatology
630 West 168th Street
New York, NY 10032
Maxine Lazarus, administrator

Provides conferences and publications about bereavement and care for the dying.

Gamblers Anonymous
2703A West Eighth Street
Los Angeles, CA 90005
Karen H., international executive secretary

Support group for gamblers and families of gamblers.

Gifted Child Society
190 Rock Road
Glen Rock, NJ 07452
Gina Ginsberg Riggs, executive director

An educational support group for gifted children and their parents.

Grandparents Anonymous
1924 Beverly
Sylvan Lake, MI 48053
Shella M. Davison, founder

Helps grandparents and grandchildren separated by divorce or family communication breakdowns.

Grief Education Institute
1780 South Bellaire Street, #132
Denver, CO 80222
Tom Lose, director

Publications concerning bereavement.

Group Project for Holocaust Survivors and Their Children
60 Riverside Drive, Apt. 11 G
New York, NY 10024
Eva Fogelman, executive officer

Offers support groups and information for families who survived the Nazi era.

Hug-A-Tree and Survive
6465 Lance Way
San Diego, CA 92120

Jacquie Beveridge, administrator
Ab Taylor, president and founder

Safety education program for kids ages 5–12 to teach them how not to get lost, and how to increase their chances of being found if they are lost.

Incest Survivors Anonymous
P.O. Box 5613
Long Beach, CA 90805

Offers discussion groups and information.

International Association of Psychosocial Rehabilitation Services
P.O. Box 278
McLean, VA 22101
Robert C. Vandiver, executive director

Provides information about rehabilitation facilities nationwide.

International Society for the Prevention of Child Abuse and Neglect
1205 Oneida Street
Denver, CO 80220
Kim Oates, president

Information and referrals concerning family welfare.

International Youth Council of Parents Without Partners
7910 Woodmont Avenue
Washington, DC 20014
L. Magnus, contact

Teenage division of Parents Without Partners; activities for the children of single parents.

Just Say No Clubs

"Just Say No" Foundation
1777 North California Boulevard, Suite 210
Walnut Creek, CA 94596
Ivy Cohen, executive director

Clubs provide information to kids so that they can resist peer pressure and other influences to use drugs.

Let's Face It

P.O. Box 711
Concord, MA 01742
Betsy Wilson, director

Support group for the facially disfigured.

Make Today Count

101½ South Union Street
Alexandria, VA 22314
Sandra Butler Whyte, executive officer

Provides information for those with terminal illnesses.

Mended Hearts

American Heart Association
7320 Greenville Avenue
Dallas, TX 75231
Joe Amato, president

Offers encouragement to children who have undergone heart surgery.

Mothers Without Custody

P.O. Box 56762
Houston, TX 77256
Janet Stockbridge, president

Advice and information for mothers who have lost or fear losing custody of their children.

National Adoption Information Exchange System

67 Irving Place
New York, NY 10003
David S. Liederman, executive director

Division of the Child Welfare League.

National AIDS Hotline

Department of Health and Human Services
200 Independence Avenue, SW
Washington, DC 20201
(800) 342-2437
Dr. Antonia Novello, surgeon general

Provides information about AIDS prevention and information on how the disease is and is not transmitted.

National Alliance for the Mentally Ill

2101 Wilson Boulevard, Suite 302
Arlington, VA 22201
Laurie M. Flynn, executive director

Organization uniting numerous self-help and advocacy groups.

National Anorexic Aid Society
5796 Karl Road
Columbus, OH 43229
Arline Iannicello, program director

Provides information and referrals for individuals suffering from anorexia, and for the families.

National Association of Anorexia Nervosa and Associated Disorders
P.O. Box 7
Highland Park, IL 60035
Vivian Meehan, executive director

Reading materials available upon request regarding anorexia and bulimia.

National Association on Drug Abuse Problems
355 Lexington Avenue
New York, NY 10017
Warren F. Pelton, president

Provides information and referrals.

National Association for Sickle Cell Disease
4221 Wilshire Boulevard, Suite 360
Los Angeles, CA 90010
Dorothye H. Boswell, executive director

Promotes research and provides information and assistance to families.

National Clearinghouse for Alcohol and Drug Information
P.O. Box 2345
Rockville, MD 20852
Dr. David Rowden, director

Provides pamphlets and information.

National Committee for the Prevention of Child Abuse
332 South Michigan Avenue
Chicago, IL 60604
Beth Waid, executive director

Provides information, referrals, and legislative lobbying.

National Council on Compulsive Gambling
c/o John Jay College of Criminal Justice
445 West 59th Street
New York, NY 10019
Sirgay Sanger, MD, president

Provides information and referrals for compulsive gamblers and their families.

National Council of Family Relations
1910 West County Road B, Suite 147
St. Paul, MN 55113
Mary Jo Czaplewski, PhD, executive director

Maintains a computerized file of family-oriented groups, nationwide.

National Federation of Parents for Drug-Free Youth
1423 North Jefferson
Springfield, MO 65802–1988
Karl Bernstein, president

National network of student groups fighting adolescent drug and alcohol use.

National Foster Parent Association
Information and Services Office
226 Kitts Drive
Houston, TX 77024
Gordon Evans, director

Promotes the rights, interests, and viewpoints of foster families.

National Foundation for Facial Reconstruction
550 First Avenue
New York, NY 10016
Robert E. Bochat, executive director

Provides research, information, and referrals for patients suffering from facial disfigurement due to accidents, burns, or problems that they were born with.

National Head Injury Foundation
333 Turnpike Road
Southborough, MA 01772
Marilyn Price Spivack, president

Provides information and research on head injuries, brain damage, and amnesia.

National Hemophilia Foundation
110 Green Street, Room 406
New York, NY 10012
Alan P. Brownstein, executive director

Provides support and information for families and those who suffer from hemophilia.

National Listen America Club
Box 100
Riverside, CA 92502
George W. French, president

Publishes material describing the effects of marijuana use.

National Mental Health Association
1021 Prince Street
Alexandria, VA 22314
Preston J. Garrison, executive director

Provides reading materials on mental health.

National Network of Runaway and Youth Services, Inc.
1400 I Street, NW, Suite 330
Washington, DC 20005
June Bucy, executive director

Network of member agencies and city, state, and regional coalitions providing services for kids. Concentrates on delinquency, drug use, pregnancy, and crisis intervention.

National Runaway Switchboard
3080 North Lincoln Avenue
Chicago, IL 60657
(800) 621–4000
John Volk, acting executive director

Parents and children can call the 800 number to make contact and leave messages.

National Self-Help Clearinghouse
Graduate School and University Center
City University of New York
33 West 42nd Street
New York, NY 10036
Dr. Frank Riessman, director

Provides information and referral for every condition and concern imaginable.

Neurotics Anonymous International Liaison
P.O. Box 466, Cleveland Park Station
Washington, DC 20008
Grover Boydston, chairman

Promotes local discussion groups for individuals who have or have had a mental illness.

North American Conference of Separated and Divorced Catholics
1100 South Goodman Street
Rochester, NY 14620
Kathleen L. Kircher, executive director

Provides support for separated and divorced parents and children.

Odyssey Institute Corporation
817 Fairfield Avenue
Bristol, CT 06604
Judianne Densen-Gerber, MD, president

Provides research, education, and advocacy programs on issues of serious concern to children.

Parents Anonymous
6733 South Sepulveda, Suite 270
Los Angeles, CA 90045
HOT LINE: (800) 421-0353
Margot Fritz, executive director

Aims to prevent child abuse through immediate support via the hot line.

Parents United
P.O. Box 952
San Jose, CA 95108
Dr. Henry Giaretto, PhD, executive director

Offers support groups for sexual molestation and drug abuse problems.

Phoenix House Foundation
164 West 74th Street
New York, NY 10023
Mitchell S. Rosenthal, MD, president

Treatment center and rehabilitation group for ex-drug users.

Phoenix Society
11 Rust Hill Road
Levittown, PA 19056
Alan Jeffry Breslau, executive director

Support for burn victims and their families.

Prison Families Anonymous
353 Fulton Avenue
Hempstead, NY 11550
Sharon Brand, executive director

Local organization interested in starting other local support groups for families with members in prison.

Rainbows
111 Tower Road
Schaumburg, IL 61073
Suzy Yehl, national director

Twelve-week support program for kids grade-school age and up who are experiencing grief following a loss.

Remarried Parents, Inc.
102–20 67th Drive
Forest Hills, NY 11375
Jack Pflaster, founder

Provides information and support for newly combined families.

Rubicon, Inc.
1300 MacTavish Avenue
Richmond, VA 23230
Van Watley, executive director

Substance abuse rehabilitation program.

Runaway Hotline
Governor's Office
P.O. Box 12428
Austin, TX 78711
(800) 231–6946
Margaret Davis, program director

Parents and children can call this organization to make contact and leave messages. Kids can call their parents and tell them they are safe without fear of being located.

Samaritans
500 Commonwealth Avenue
Boston, MA 02215
Shirley Karnovsky, executive director

Suicide prevention service and information.

Search Reports, Inc./A Central Registry of the Missing
396 Route 17, North
Hasbrouck Heights, NJ 07604
(800) 526–4603
Charles A. Sutherland, president

Information on missing children for parents, and also a contact for runaway children who wish to get in touch with their parents.

Self-Help Center
1600 Dodge Avenue, Suite S–122
Evanston, IL 60201
Daryl Isenberg, PhD, acting director

Clearinghouse for information and referrals.

Single Parent Resource Center
1165 Broadway, Room 504
New York, NY 10001
Suzanne Jones, executive director

Provides support and information for various single-parent organizations.

Sisterhood of Black Single Mothers
1360 Fulton Street, Suite 423
Brooklyn, NY 11216
Daphne Busby, executive director

Self-help organization that also works with the children of black single mothers.

Stepfamily Foundation, Inc.
333 West End Avenue
New York, NY 10024
Jeannette Lofas, executive director

Offers information and counseling for newly created families.

Students Against Driving Drunk (SADD)
P.O. Box 800
Marlboro, MA 01752
Robert Anastas, executive director/founder

Organization of students united to combat drunk driving. Provides a community awareness program; promotes the use of

the student-parent contract and the party guide.

Students to Offset Peer Pressure (STOPP)
STOPP Consulting Services
P.O. Box 103
Hudson, NH 03051–0103
Peter M. Jean, executive director

Group promoting a drug-free environment for kids in preschool through high school.

Toughlove
P.O. Box 1069
Doylestown, PA 18901
Gwen Olitsky, managing director

Group that deals with "problem" children with a mixture of discipline, forgiveness, and understanding.

Woman's Christian Temperance Union
1730 Chicago Avenue
Evanston, IL 60201
Frances Bateman, national executive director

Sponsors four youth groups advocating total abstinence as the most effective way of avoiding alcohol and drug abuse.

Youth Suicide National Center
204 East Second Avenue, Suite 203
San Mateo, CA 94401
Charlotte Rose, executive director

Coordinates and mobilizes efforts to prevent youth suicide, starting with kids as young as one year old.

Youth to Youth
CompDrug
700 Bryden Road
Columbus, OH 43215
Theresa Garrison, director

Sponsors a puppet show "Proud to Be Drug Free" for elementary school students. Also sponsors training conferences for kids/adults working in anti-drug programs.

WHO'S IN CHARGE HERE AND IN THE REST OF THE WORLD

The first part of this category is the federal government of the United States—the president and vice-president first, followed by a list of federal agencies and departments. Following that is a list of the United States and their governors. The final category is a list of countries and their rulers. Each list is in alphabetical order.

Bush, George Herbert Walker
The White House
1600 Pennsylvania Avenue
Washington, DC 20500
President of the United States

Quayle, J. Danforth
Admiral House
34th and Massachusetts
Washington, DC 20005
Vice-president of the United States

Administration for Children, Youth and Families
Office of Human Development Services, US Department of Health & Human Services
Washington, DC 20201
Wade Horn, commissioner

The focal agency for the federal government serving children and families.

Department of Agriculture
The Mall, 12th & 14th Streets
Washington, DC 20250
Edward Madigan, Secretary of Agriculture

Department of Commerce
14th Street between Constitution & E Street, NW
Washington, DC 20230
Robert Mosbacher, Secretary of Commerce

Department of Defense
The Pentagon
Washington, DC 20301
Richard B. Cheney, Secretary of Defense

Department of Education
400 Maryland Avenue, SW
Washington, DC 20202
Lamar Alexander, Secretary of
Education

Department of Energy
1000 Independence Avenue, SW
Washington, DC 20585
James D. Watkins, Secretary of
Energy

**Department of Health and
Human Services**
200 Independence Avenue, SW
Washington, DC 20201
Louis W. Sullivan, Secretary of
Health and Human Services

**Department of Housing and
Urban Development**
451 7th Street, SW
Washington, DC 20410
Jack Kemp, Secretary of Housing
and Urban Development

Department of Justice
Constitution Avenue and 10th
Street, NW
Washington, DC 20530
William P. Barr, Attorney General

Department of Labor
200 Constitution Avenue, NW
Washington, DC 20210
Lynn Martin, Secretary of Labor

Department of State
2201 C Street, NW
Washington, DC 20520
James A. Baker, Secretary of
State

Department of the Air Force
The Pentagon
Washington, DC 20330
Donald B. Rice, Secretary of the
Air Force

Department of the Army
The Pentagon
Washington, DC 20310
Michael P. W. Stone, Secretary of
the Army

Department of the Interior
C Street between 18th & 19th
Streets, NW
Washington, DC 20240
Manuel Lujan, Secretary of the
Interior

Department of the Navy
The Pentagon
Washington, DC 20350
H. Lawrence Garrett III, Secretary of the Navy

Department of the Treasury
1500 Pennsylvania Avenue, NW
Washington, DC 20220
Nicholas F. Brady, Secretary of
the Treasury

Department of Transportation
400 7th Street, SW
Washington, DC 20590
Samuel K. Skinner, Secretary of
Transportation

Department of Veterans Affairs
810 Vermont Avenue, NW
Washington, DC 20420
Edward J. Derwinski, Secretary
of Veterans Affairs

Federal Aviation Administration (FAA)
400 7th Street, SW
Washington, DC 20590
James Busey, chairman

Governs all air travel in the US.

Federal Bureau of Investigation (FBI)
Ninth Street and Pennsylvania Avenue
Washington, DC 20535
William Steele Sessions, director

National "police force"

Federal Communications Commission (FCC)
1919 M Street, NW
Washington, DC 20554
Alfred C. Sikes, director

Government organization that oversees all communications, including radio and television.

Federal Trade Commission (FTC)
Pennsylvania Avenue at 6th Street, NW
Washington, DC 20580
Daniel Oliver, chairman

Government commission responsible for the US trading of products with foreign countries.

Food & Drug Administration (FDA)
5600 Fishers Lane
Rockville, MD 20857
Frank E. Young, commissioner

US Government department that oversees what drugs are marketed in the US and what is safe to eat.

United States Committee for UNICEF
331 East 38th Street
New York, NY 11235
Lawrence Bruce, president

Promotes fundraising among kids for other kids who need help. Includes the annual Halloween campaign.

United States Supreme Court
US Supreme Court Building
One First Street NE
Washington, DC 20543
William H. Rehnquist, chief justice
Harry A. Blackmun, Anthony M. Kennedy, Sandra Day O'Connor, Antonin Scalia, David H. Souter, John Paul Stevens, Clarence Thomas and Byron R. White, associate justices

U.S. Marine Corps
Arlington Annex
Washington, DC 20380
General Carl E. Mundy, Jr., commandant

Alabama
State Capitol
Montgomery, AL 36130
Guy Hunt, governor

Alaska
P.O. Box A
Juneau, AK 99811
Walter J. Hickel, governor

Arizona
State House
Phoenix, AZ 85007
Fife Symington, governor

Arkansas
State Capitol
Little Rock, AR 72201
Bill Clinton, governor

California
State Capitol
Sacramento, CA 95814
Pete Wilson, governor

Colorado
136 State Capitol
Denver, CO 80203
Roy Romer, governor

Connecticut
State Capitol
Hartford, CT 06106
Lowell Weicker, Jr., governor

Delaware
Legislative Hall
Dover, DE 19901
Michael N. Castle, governor

Florida
State Capitol
Tallahassee, FL 32399–0001
Lawton Chiles, governor

Georgia
State Capitol
Atlanta, GA 30334
Zell Miller, governor

Hawaii
State Capitol
Honolulu, HI 96813
John D. Waihee, governor

Idaho
State Capitol
Boise, ID 83720
Cecil D. Andrus, governor

Illinois
State Capitol
Springfield, Illinois 62706
James Edgar, governor

Indiana
Room 206, Statehouse
Indianapolis, Indiana 46204
Evan Bayh, governor

Iowa
State Capitol
Des Moines, Iowa 50319
Terry E. Branstad, governor

Kansas
State House
Topeka, Kansas 66612
Joan Finney, governor

Kentucky
State Capitol
Frankfort, KY 40601
Brereton Jones, governor

Louisiana
State Capitol
Baton Rouge, LA 70904
Edwin Edwards, governor

Maine
State House
Augusta, ME 04333
John R. McKernan, Jr., governor

Maryland
State House
Annapolis, MD 21404
William Donald Schaefer, governor

Massachusetts
State House
Boston, MA 02133
William F. Weld, governor

Michigan
State Capitol
Lansing, MI 48909
John Engler, governor

Minnesota
State Capitol
St. Paul, MN 55155
Arne Carlson, governor

Mississippi
P.O. Box 139
Jackson, MS 39205
Kirk Fordice, governor

Missouri
State Capitol
Jefferson City, MO 65101
John D. Ashcroft, governor

Montana
State Capitol
Helena, MT 59620
Stan Stephens, governor

Nebraska
State Capitol
Lincoln, NE 69509
Ben Nelson, governor

Nevada
State Capitol
Carson City, NV 89710
Robert Miller, governor

New Hampshire
State House, Room 208
Concord, NH 03301
Judd Gregg, governor

New Jersey
State House, Office of the Governor, CN-001
Trenton, NJ 08625
James J. Florio, governor

New Mexico
State Capitol
Santa Fe, NM 87503
Bruce King, governor

New York
State Capitol
Albany, NY 12224
Mario M. Cuomo, governor

North Carolina
State Capitol
Raleigh, NC 27603
James G. Martin, Jr., governor

North Dakota
600 East Boulevard, State Capitol, Ground Floor
Bismarck, ND 58505
George A. Sinner, governor

Ohio
State House
Columbus, OH 43215
George V. Voinovich, governor

Oklahoma
State Capitol, Room 212
Oklahoma City, OK 73105
David Walters, governor

Oregon
State Capitol
Salem, OR 97310
Barbara Roberts, governor

Pennsylvania
State Capitol
Harrisburg, PA 17120
Robert P. Casey, governor

Rhode Island
State House
Providence, RI 02903
Bruce Sundlun, governor

South Carolina
State House
Columbia, SC 29211
Carroll A. Campbell, Jr., governor

South Dakota
State Capitol
Pierre, SD 57501
George S. Mickelson, governor

Tennessee
State Capitol
Nashville, TN 37219
Ned Ray McWherter, governor

Texas
State Capitol
Austin, TX 78711
Ann Richards, governor

Utah
210 State Capitol
Salt Lake City, UT 84114
Norman H. Bangerter, governor

Vermont
Pavilion Office Building
Montpelier, VT 05602
Howard Dean, governor

Virginia
State Capitol
Richmond, VA 23219
L. Douglas Wilder, governor

Washington
State Capitol
Olympia, WA 98504
Booth Gardner, governor

West Virginia
State Capitol
Charleston, WV 25305
Gaston Caperton, governor

Wisconsin
State Capitol
Madison, WI 53707
Tommy G. Thompson, governor

Wyoming
State Capitol
Cheyenne, WY 82002
Mike Sullivan, governor

Afghanistan
People's Democratic Party of Afghanistan
Kabul, Afghanistan
Sigbatullah Mojadedi, president

Albania
Office of the President
Tirana, Albania
Ramiz Alia, president

Algeria
Presidence de la Republique
El Moradia, Algiers, Algeria
Chadli Bendjedid, president

Angola
Gabinete de Presidente
Luanda, Angola
Jose Eduardo dos Santos, president

Antigua & Barbuda
Office of the Governor General
St. John's, Antigua, West Indies
Sir Wilfred E. Jacobs, governor general

Argentina
Casa de Gobierno
Balcarce 50, 1064 Buenos Aires
Argentina
Carlos Saúl Menem, president

Australia
Parliament House
Canberra, A.C.T., Australia
Robert J. L. Hawke, prime minister

Austria
Präsidentschaftskanzlei
Hofburg, 1014 Vienna, Austria
Kurt Waldheim, president

Bahamas
P.O. Box N10846
Nassau, Bahamas
Sir Henry Milton Taylor, governor general

Bahrain
Rifa's Palace
Manama, Bahrain
Shiekh Isa bin Sulman al-Khalifa, emir

Bangladesh
Office of the Prime Minister
Dhaka, Bangladesh
Begum Khaleda Zia, prime minister

Barbados
Government House
Bridgetown, Barbados
Dame Nita Barrow, governor general

Belgium
16 rue de la Loi
1000 Brussels, Belgium
Wilfried Martens, prime minister

Belize
c/o House of Representatives
Belmopan, Belize
Rt. Hon. George Cadle Price, prime minister

Benin
Office of the President
Cotonou, Benin
Nicephore Soglo, president

Bhutan
Royal Palace
Thimphu, Bhutan
King Jigme Singye Wangchuk, ruler

Bolivia
Palacio de Gobierno
Plaza Murillo
La Paz, Bolivia
Jaime Paz Zamora, president

Bophuthatswana
Department of the Presidency
Private Bag X2005
Mafikeng, Bophuthatswana,
    South Africa
Kgosi Lucas Magope, president

Botswana
State House
Private Bag 001, Gaborone
Botswana
Quett Ketumile Joni Masire,
    president

Brazil
Oficina del Presidente
Palacio de Planalto
Praca dos Tres Poderes, 70.150
    Brasilia, Brazil
Fernando Affonso Collor de
    Mello, president

Brunei Darussalam
Istana Darul Hana
Brunei
H. M. Sultan Sir Mud Hassanal
    Bolkia Mu'isuddin Waddaulah,
    ruler

Bulgaria
Office of the Prime Minister
Sofia, Bulgaria
Dmitar Popov, prime minister

Burkina Faso
Office of the President
Ouagadougou, Burkina Faso
Blaise Campaore, chairman of
    the Popular Front

Burundi
Office of the President and Na-
    tional Defense
Bujumbura, Burundi
Major Pierre Buyoya, president

Cambodia
(Provisional, self-styled govern-
    ment)
Pyon yang, Democratic People's
    Republic of Korea (headquar-
    ters)
Prince Sandech Preah Norodom
    Sihanouk, president

Cameroon
Office of the President
Yaounde, Cameroon
Paul Biya, president

Canada
Office of the Prime Minister
Langevin Block, 80 Wellington
    Street
Ottawa K1A 042
Canada
Brian Mulroney, prime minister

Cape Verde
Office of the President
Cidade de Praia
Sao Tiago, Cape Verde
Antonio Mascarenhas Monteiro,
    president

Central African Republic
Presidence de la Republique
Bangui, Central African Republic
General Andre Kolingba, presi-
    dent

Chad
Office of the President
N'Djamena, Chad
Colonel Idriss Deby, president

Chile
Oficina de Presidente
Palacio de la Moneda
Santiago, Chile
Patricio Aylwin, president

China (People's Republic of)
Office of the President
Beijing, People's Republic of
China
General Yang Shangkun, president

Ciskei
c/o Head of State
Zwelitsha, Ciskei, South Africa
Brigadier General Oupa Ggozo,
head of state

Colombia
Office of the President
Casa de Narino
Carrera 8A, No 7–26
Bogota, Colombia
Cesar Gaviria Trujillo, president

Comoros
Office of the President
Moroni, Comoros
Said Mohammed Djohar, president

Congo
Office du President
Comite Miltaire du Parti
Congolais du Travail
Brazzaville, Congo People's
Republic
Colonel Denis Sassou-
Nguessou, president

Costa Rica
Casa Presidencial
Apdo 520 Zapote
San Jose, Costa Rica
Rafael Angel Calderon Fournier,
president

Côte d'Ivoire
Presidence de la Republique
Abidjan, Côte d'Ivoire
Felix Houphouet-Boigny, president

Cuba
Palacio del Gobierno
Havana, Cuba
Fidel Castro Ruz, head of state
and president of council of
state

Cyprus
Presidential Palace
Nicosia, Cyprus
Dr. George Vassiliou, president

Czechoslovakia
Kancelar prezidenta republiky
11908 Praha-Hradcany
Prague, Czechoslovakia
Vaclav Havel, president

Denmark
Prime Minister's Office
Christianborg, Prins Jorgens Gaardii
1218 Copenhagen K, Denmark
Poul Holmskov Schluter, prime
minister

Djibouti
Presidence de la Republique
Djibouti, Republic of Djibouti
Hassan Gouled Aptidon, president

Dominica
The President's Office
Roseau, Commonwealth of
    Dominica, West Indies
Sir Clarence Seignoret, president

Dominican Republic
Oficina del Presidente
Santo Domingo, D.N., Domini-
    can Republic
Joaquin Balaguer Ricardo, presi-
    dent

Ecuador
Office of the President
Palacio Nacional
Garcia Moreno 1043
Quito, Ecuador
Rodrigo Borja Cevallos, presi-
    dent

Egypt
Presidential Palace
Abdeen, Cairo
Egypt
Hosni Mubarak, president

El Salvador
Oficina del Presidente
San Salvador, El Salvador
Alfredo Cristiani, president

Equatorial Guinea
Oficina del Presidente
Malabo, Equatorial Guinea
Colonel Teodoro Obiang
    Nguema Mbasogo, president

Ethiopia
c/o Ethiopian People's Revolu-
    tionary Democratic Front
Addis Ababa, Ethiopia
Meles Zenawi, president

Fiji
Office of the President
Suva, Fiji
Ratu Sir Penaia Kanatabatu
    Ganilau, president

Finland
Presidential Palace
Helsinki, Finland
Mauno Henrik Koivisto, presi-
    dent

France
Palais de l'Elysee
55–57 rue du Faubourg Saint-
    Honoré
75008 Paris
France
François Maurice Marie Mitter-
    rand, president

Gabon
Presidence de la Republique
Boite Postale 546
Libreville, Gabon
Omar (Albert-Bernard) Bongo,
    president

Gambia
Office of the President
Banjul, the Gambia
Sir Dawda K. Jawara, president

Germany
Marbacher Strasse 11
6700 Ludwigshafen/Rhein
Federal Republic of Germany
Helmut Kohl, chancellor

Ghana
Office of the Head of State
The Castle
Accra, Ghana

Flight Lt. Jerry John Rawlings, chairman of the Provisional Defense Council

Greece
Office of the President
Odos Zalokosta 10
Athens, Greece
Konstantinos G. Karamanlis, president

Grenada
Governor General's House
St. George's, Grenada
Sir Paul Scoon, governor general

Guatemala
Oficina del Presidente
Guatemala City, Guatemala
Jorge Serrano Elias, president

Guinea
Office du President
Conakry, Guinea
Brig. Gen. Lansana Conte, president

Guinea-Bissau
Conselho de Estado
Bissau, Guinea-Bissau
Joao Bernardo Vieira, president of the Council of State

Guyana
Office of the President
New Garden Street
Georgetown, Guyana
Hugh Desmond Hoyte, president

Haiti
Office of the President
Port-au-Prince, Haiti
Rev. Jean-Bertrand Aristide, president

Honduras
Casa Presidencial
6a Avda, la Calle
Tegucigalpa, Honduras
Rafael L. Callejas, president

Hungary
Office of the President
1055 Budapest
Kossuth Lajos ter 1
Hungary
Arpad Goncz, president

Iceland
Office of the President
Reykjavik, Iceland
Mrs. Vigdis Finnbogadottir, president

India
Lok Sabha
New Delhi, India
P. V. Narasimha Rao, prime minister

Indonesia
Office of the President
15 Jalan Merdeka Utara
Jakarta, Indonesia
Suharto, president

Iran
c/o Islamic Republican Party
Dr. Al Shariati Avenue
Teheran, Iran
Hashemi Rafsanjani, president

Iraq
Revolutionary Command Council
Baghdad, Iraq
Saddam Hussein, president

Ireland
Abbeville, Kinsealy
County Dublin, Ireland
Charles J. Haughey, Taoiseach
(prime minister)

Israel
Office of the Prime Minister
Hakirya, Ruppin Street
Jerusalem, Israel
Yitzhak Shamir, prime minister

Italy
Palazzo del Quirinale
00187 Rome
Italy
Francesco Cossiga, premier

Jamaica
People's National Party
89 Old Hope Road
Kingston 6
Jamaica
Michael Manley, prime minister

Japan
House of Representatives
Tokyo, Japan
Kilchi Miyazawa, prime minister

Jordan
Royal Palace
Amman, Jordan
King Hussein I, ruler

Kenya
Office of the President
P.O. Box 30510
Nairobi, Kenya
Daniel arap Moi, president

Kiribati
Office of the President
Tarawa, Kiribati
Ieremia Tabai, president

Korea (North)
Office of the President
Pyongyang
Democratic People's Republic of
Korea
Marshal Kim Il-Sung, president

Korea (South)
Chong Wa Dae
1 Sejongno, Chougnogu
Seoul 110–050, Republic of
Korea
Roh Tae Woo, president

Kuwait
Sief Palace
Amiry Diwan, Kuwait
Sheik Jaber al-Ahmad al-Sabah,
emir

Laos
Office of the President
Vientiane, Laos
Phoumi Vongvichit, president

Latvia
Presidium of Latvian Supreme
Soviet
Riga, Latvian SSR
Anatolijs Gorbunovs, president

Lebanon
Office of the President
Beirut, Lebanon
Elias Hrawi, president

Lesotho
The Military Council
Maseru, Lesotho
Colonel E. P. Ramaema, head of
  government

Liberia
Office of the President
Monrovia, Liberia
Amos Sawyer, president

Libya
Office of the President
Tripoli, Libya
Colonel Muammar el Qaddafi,
  head of state

Liechtenstein
Schloss Vaduz
Principality of Liechtenstein
Prince Hans Adam II, ruler

Lithuania
Office of the President
Supreme Council of Lithuania
Vilnius, Lithuania SSR
Vytautas Landsbergis, president

Luxembourg
Grand Ducal Palace
2013 Luxembourg
Grand Duke Jean Benoit
  Guillaume Marie Robert Louis
  Antoine Adolphe Marc
  D'Aviano, ruler

Madagascar
Presidence de la Republique

Antananarivo, Madagascar
Didier Ratsiraka, president and
  head of state

Malawi
Office of the President
Private Bag 388
Capital City, Lilongwe 3
Malawi
Hastings Kamuzu Banda, president

Malaysia
Office of the Prime Minister
Jalan Dato Onn
Kuala Lumpur, Malaysia
D.S. Mahathir bin Mohamad,
  prime minister

Maldives
Office of the President
Male, Maldives
Maumoon-Abdul Gayoom,
  president

Mali
c/o Cabinet du President
Comité militaire du liberation
  nationale
B.P. 1463, Bamako, Mali
Lt. Col. Amadou Toumani Toure,
  president

Malta
Office of the President
The Palace
Valletta, Malta
Dr. Vincent Tabone, president

Mauritania
Presidence de la Republique
B.P. 184, Nouakchott
Mauritania

Col. Maaouye Ould Sidi Ahmed Taya, chief of state and head of government

Mauritius
Government House
Port Louis, Mauritius
Aneerood Jugnauth, prime minister

Mexico
Palacio de Gobierno
Mexico City, DF, Mexico
Carlos Salinas de Gortari, president

Monaco
Plais de Monaco
Boite Postal 518
98015 Monte Carlo
Monaco
Prince Rainier III, ruler

Mongolia
Presidential Palace
Ulan Bator
Mongolian People's Republic
Punsalmaagiyn Ochirbat, chairman of the presidium of the Great People's Khural

Morocco
Royal Palace
Rabat, Morocco
King Hassan II, ruler

Mozambique
Office of the President
Avda Julius Nyerere
Maputo, Mozambique
Joaquim Chissano, president

Myanmar
Office of the Prime Minister
Yangon, Myanmar
General Saw Maung, head of state (chairman)

Namibia
c/o Office of the President
Namibia
Sam Shafilshuna Nujoma, president

Nauru
c/o Parliament House
Nauru, Central Pacific
Bernard Dowiyogo, president

Nepal
Narayanhity Royal Palace
Kathmandu, Nepal
King Birendra Bir Bikram Shah Deva, ruler

The Netherlands
Office of the Prime Minister
The Hague, Netherlands
Ruud Lubbers, premier

New Zealand
Prime Minister's Office
Parliament Buildings
Wellington, New Zealand
James Brendan Bolger, prime minister

Nicaragua
Oficina del Presidente
Managua, Nicaragua
Violeta Barrios de Chamorro, president

Niger
Office of the Chairman of the
High Council for National Ori-
entation
Niamey, Niger
General Ali Saibou, chief of state

Nigeria
Office of the President
Dodan Barracks
Ikoyi, Lagos
Nigeria
General Ibrahim Badamasi
Babangida, president

Norway
Royal Palace
Oslo, Norway
King Harald V, sovereign

Oman
The Palace
Muscat, Sultanate of Oman
Qaboos bin Said, sultan

Pakistan
Office of the President
Constitution Avenue
Islamabad, Pakistan
Ghulam Ishaq Khan, president

Panama
Oficina del Presidente
Valija 50, Panama 1
Panama
Guillermo Endara Galimany,
president

Papua New Guinea
The Prime Minister's Office
Government Buildings
Port Moresby

Papua, New Guinea
Rabbie Namaliu, prime minister

Paraguay
Casa Presidencial
Avenida Mariscal Lopez
Asunción, Paraguay
General Andres Rodriguez, presi-
dent

Peru
Office of the President
Lima, Peru
Alberto Kenyo Fujimori, presi-
dent

The Philippines
Office of the President
Malacanong
Manila, Philippines
Corazon C. Aquino, president

Poland
Kancelaria Presydenta RP
Ul Wiejska 4/8
00-902 Warsaw
Poland
Lech Walesa, president

Portugal
Presidencia da Republica
Palacio de Belem
1300 Lisbon
Portugal
Mario Soares, president

Qatar
The Royal Palace
Doha, Qatar
Sheikh Khalifa bin Hamad al-
Thani, emir

Romania
Office of the President
Bucharest, Romania
Ion Iliescu, president

Russia
The Kremlin
Moscow, Russia
Boris Yeltsin, president

Rwanda
Presidence de la Republique
Kigali, Rwanda
Major General Juvenal Haby-
arimana, president

San Marino
Grand and General Council
San Marino, San Marino
*Two co-regents are selected
every six months by the Grand
and General Council.*

Sao Tome and Principe
Office of the President
Sao Tome, Sao Tome and Prin-
cipe
Miguel Anjos de Cunha Lisboa
Trovoada, president

Saudi Arabia
Royal Diwan
Riyadh, Saudi Arabia
King Fahd Ibn Abdul Aziz, ruler

Senegal
Office of the President
Avenue Roume
BP 168, Dakar
Senegal
Abdou Diouf, president

Seychelles
The State House
Victoria, Mahe
Seychelles
France-Albert Rene, president

Sierra Leone
Office of the President
Freetown, Sierra Leone
Major General Joseph Saidu
Momoh, president

Singapore
Prime Minister's Office
Istana, Singapore 0923
Goh Chok Tong, prime minister

Solomon Islands
Office of the Prime Minister
P.O. Box G01
Honiara, Guadalcanal
Solomon Islands
Solomon Mamaloni, prime min-
ister

Somalia
Office of the President
Mogadishu, Somalia
Ali Mahdi Mohammed, presi-
dent

South Africa
Tuynhuys
Cape Town 8000
South Africa
Frederik Willem de Klerk, presi-
dent

Spain
Palacio de la Zarzuela
Madrid, Spain
King Juan Carlos I, ruler

Sri Lanka
Office of the President
Republic Square
Colombo 1
Sri Lanka
Ranasinghe Premadasa, president

St. Kitts and Nevis
Office of the Prime Minister
Basseterre, St. Kitts, West Indies
Kennedy Alphonse Simmonds, prime minister

St. Lucia
Office of the Prime Minister
Castries, St. Lucia
John George Melvin Compton, prime minister

St. Vincent and The Grenadines
Prime Minister's Office
Kingstown, St. Vincent
James Fitzallen, prime minister

Sudan
Revolutionary Command Council
Khartoum, Sudan
Brigadier Omar Hassam Ahmed Bashir, prime minister

Suriname
Office of the President
Paramaribo, Suriname
Johan Kraag, president

Swaziland
Royal Palace
Mbabane, Swaziland
King Mswati III, ruler

Sweden
Statsradsbereduingen
10333 Stockholm
Sweden
Ingvar Gösta Carlsson, prime minister

Switzerland
Office of the President
Bundeshaus West
Bundesgassse, 3003 Berne
Switzerland
Flavio Cotti, president

Syria
Office of the President
Damascus, Syria
Lieutenant General Hafiz al-Assad, president

Taiwan
Office of the President
Taipei, Taiwan, Republic of China
Li Teng-hui, president

Tanzania
c/o Office of the President
Dar-es-Salaam, United Republic of Tanzania
Ali Hassan Mwinyi, president

Thailand
Chitralada Villa
Bangkok, Thailand
King Bhumibol Adulyadej, ruler

Togo
Presidence de la Republique
Lomé, Togo
Kokou Koffigoh, president

Tonga
The Palace
P.O. Box 6
Nuku'alofa, Tonga
King Taufa'ahau Tupou IV,
    sovereign

Transkei
Office of the President
Transkei, South Africa
Chief Tutor Nyangilizwe
    Ndamase, president

Trinidad and Tobago
President's House
St. Ann's, Trinidad and Tobago
Noor Mohammed Hassanali,
    president

Tunisia
Presidence de la Republique
Tunis, Tunisia
General Zine al-Abidine Ben Ali,
    president

Turkey
Cumhurbaskanligi Kosku
Cankaya, Ankara, Turkey
Turgut Ozal, president

Tuvalu
Office of the Prime Minister
Funafuti, Tuvalu
Bikenibeu Paeniu, prime min-
    ister

Uganda
Office of the President
Kampala, Uganda
Yoweri Kaguta Museveni, presi-
    dent

United Arab Emirates
Amiti Palace
Abu Dhabi, United Arab Emirates
Sheikh Zayed Bin Sultan Al-
    Nahayan, president

United Kingdom
10 Downing Street
London S.W.1, England
United Kingdom
John Major, prime minister

Uruguay
Oficina del Presidente
Montevideo, Uruguay
Luis Alberto Lacalle, president

Vanuatu
Office of the President
Port Vila, Vanuatu
Fred Timakata, president

Vatican City State
Apostolic Palace
Vatican City
His Holiness Pope John Paul II
    (Karol Wojtyla), ruler

Venda
Council of National Unity
Thohoyandou, Venda, South
    Africa
Colonel Gabriel Mutheiwana
    Ramushwana, chairman of
    the Council of National Unity

Venezuela
c/o Oficina del Presidente
Palacio de Miraflores
Caracas, Venezuela
Carlos Andres Perez Rodriguez,
    president

Vietnam
c/o Council of Ministers
Bac Thao, Hanoi
Vietnam
Vo Chi Cong, president

Western Samoa
Government House
Vailima, Apia
Western Samoa, South Pacific
Malietoa Tanumafili II, head of
   state

Yemen
Office of the President
San'a', Republic of Yemen
Ali Abdullah Saleh, president

Yugoslavia
Federal Executive Council
11070 Belgrade, buli Lenjina 2
Yugoslavia
Stipe Mesic, president

Zaire
Presidence de la Republique
Kinshasa, Zaire
Mobutu Sese Seko, president

Zambia
State House
P.O. Box 135
Lusaka, Zambia
Kenneth David Kaunda, presi-
   dent

Zimbabwe
Office of the President
Harare, Zimbabwe
Robert Mugabe, executive presi-
   dent

WRITE TO ME

I hope you like writing letters half as much as I like reading them. Please feel free to send me your ideas, comments, drawings, whatever.

Here are a couple of rules if you write to me:

- If you want me to respond, remember to include a self-addressed stamped envelope. The reasons are both time and cost. It's the only way I can answer your mail; so unfortunately I've had to draw the line. No self-addressed stamped envelope, no reply. No exceptions.
- I need your comments. I would love to hear any success stories that you have as a result of the book, and any ideas for additional people who may have been overlooked, but who could be included in future editions.
- Many people write to me to request addresses of people not listed in the book. As much as I would like to, I simply cannot open up this can of worms. Requests for additional addresses are carefully noted and considered for future editions.
- Most important, send me a photo. That's right, enclose a photo of yourself. After all, from the photo on the back cover you know what I look like and I'm rather curious to see you. Receiving a photo from someone who writes adds an entire new dimension to the letter.

I look forward to reading your letter.

Michael Levine
KID'S ADDRESS BOOK
8730 Sunset Boulevard, 6th Floor
Los Angeles, CA 90069

Author Michael Levine announces

The *Kid's Address Book*
Letter-writing Contest

Writing *is* its own reward, but as further incentive to get kids to write, we're announcing the *Kid's Address Book* Letter-writing Contest. There are three age categories: 5–8, 9–11, and 12–14. Here's how to enter:

- *RULES:* Send in a copy of a letter written to someone listed in *The Kid's Address Book,* 200 words maximum. Letters will be judged on style, content, originality, sincerity, and enthusiasm.
- *JUDGES:* A distinguished panel of judges, including author Michael Levine, will determine the winners.
- *PRIZES:* Best letter-writers in each category will win a trophy and writing certificate, along with $200 cash and other assorted prizes.

Send a copy of your letter(s) to: Michael Levine, *Kid's Address Book*, 8730 Sunset Blvd., 6th Floor, Los Angeles, CA 90069

All entries must arrive no later than February 28, 1993. Contest drawing will be held on March 31, 1993. Schools and organizations are encouraged to participate with parents' and teachers' supervision.

Remember, one person who writes to another is more powerful than ten thousand who remain silent.
Good luck!

OFFICIAL CONTEST RULES

1. On an official entry form or a 3″ by 5″ piece of paper, hand print your name, address, telephone number, and age and mail entry along with a copy of your letter to one of the persons or organiza-

tions listed in the *Kid's Address Book*, in a hand-addressed envelope (#10), to *Kid's Address Book* CONTEST, Attn: Michael Levine, c/o *Kid's Address Book*, 8730 Sunset Boulevard, 6th floor, Los Angeles, California 90069. Only one entry per person.

2. Entries must be received no later than February 28, 1993. Not responsible for misdirected or lost mail.

3. The letter accompanying your entry should be to a person or organization listed in the *Kid's Address Book* and should not be more than 200 words in length. There will be prizes for letters in three age categories: ages 5–8, 9–11, and 12–14, and will be judged on style, content, originality, uniqueness of message, and enthusiasm.

4. The winner in each age category will win a prize of $200, a trophy, and may have his or her letter published in the next edition of the *Kid's Address Book*. The winner will be determined on March 31, 1993. In the event there are an insufficient number of entries that meet the maximum requirements of the judges, the sponsor reserves the right not to award all prizes.

5. This contest is open to all US and Canadian (excluding Quebec) residents. Prizes won by a minor will be awarded to the minor's parent or guardian. No purchase necessary. Void where prohibited by law. Employees and their families of the Putnam Berkley Group, Inc., MCA, Matsushita Electric Industrial Company, Ltd., Levine, Schneider, their respective affiliates, retailers, distributors, advertising, promotion, and production agencies are not eligible to participate. Taxes on any prize awarded are the sole responsibility of the prize winner, who may be required to sign a statement of eligibility. The names and likenesses of the winner and the prize-winning letter may be used for promotional purposes.

6. For the name of the prize winner send a stamped, self-addressed envelope to: Michael Levine, c/o *Kid's Address Book*, 8730 Sunset Boulevard, 6th floor, Los Angeles, California 90069

OFFICIAL ENTRY FORM:

To enter the contest, fill in the information below and return it to:

THE KID'S ADDRESS BOOK CONTEST
Attn: Michael Levine
KID'S ADDRESS BOOK
8730 Sunset Boulevard—6th floor
Los Angeles CA 90069

No purchase necessary. Void where prohibited by law. For complete rules, see pages 189-190.

NAME _____

ADDRESS _____

CITY/STATE _____

PHONE NO. _____ **AGE** _____

Mail this entry form or a 3″ by 5″ piece of paper along with a copy of the letter to a person or organization listed in the book no later than February 28, 1993.

Michael Levine's comprehensive address books provide access to the inaccessible.

THE ADDRESS BOOK
Used by everyone from the White House staff to Barbara Walters, this volume contains the most confidential mailing addresses of thousands of the world's most powerful, interesting, and influential people.

THE ENVIRONMENTAL ADDRESS BOOK
A powerful tool to help concerned citizens take part in the fight to save the planet, with listings for more than 2,000 leading environmental figures and organizations, concerned celebrities, and some of the worst polluters.

THE KID'S ADDRESS BOOK
A fun-filled, information-packed collection of addresses geared specifically to the needs and interests of children aged six through fifteen.

These books are available at your bookstore or wherever books are sold, or for your convenience, we'll send them directly to you. Just call 1-800-631-8571, or fill out the coupon below and send it to:

The Putnam Publishing Group
390 Murray Hill Parkway, Dept. B
East Rutherford, NJ 07073

		Price	
		U.S.	Canada
_____The Address Book	399-51621-2	$ 9.95	$12.95
_____The Environmental Address Book	399-51660-3	14.95	19.50
_____The Kid's Address Book	399-51783-9	8.95	11.75
	Subtotal	$ _____	
	Postage and handling*	$ _____	
	Sales tax (CA, NJ, NY, PA)	$ _____	
	Total amount due	$ _____	

Payable in U.S. funds (no cash orders accepted). $15.00 minimum on credit card orders.
*Postage & handling: $2.50 for 1 book, 75¢ for each additional book up to a maximum of $6.25.

Enclosed is my ☐ check ☐ money order
Please charge my ☐ Visa ☐ MasterCard ☐ American Express

Card # _____ Expiration date _____
Signature as on charge card _____
Name _____
Address _____ City _____ State ____ Zip _____

Please allow six weeks for delivery. Prices subject to change without notice.
Source key #42